It's About Time

(Millions of Copies Sold for Dad)

Mark Connor

Acknowledgements

Special thanks to:

Dan Flynn, Editorial Advisor and Cover Concept

Kelly Rowe, Legal Advisor

Tony Zirnhelt, Printer Services and Advisor

Andrew Grimes, Editor

Lana Mowdy, Copy Editor

Julie Tilka, Designer

Eric C. Keast, Cover Artist
Original painting, *"It's About Time"*

Connemara Patch Press, LLC, Saint Paul, Minnesota

Four poems appearing in this story, *My Now Departed Brother, Upon the Finishing of My House Fried Rice, Halfway Around,* and *Life So Simple* were previously anthologized by Gabriel's Horn Press.

Copyright © 2024

All rights reserved. No part of this book may be reproduced in any form without the permission of Mark Connor or Connemara Patch Press, LLC.

ISBN Number ISBN: 979-8-9904917-0-0

Printed in the United States of America.

*To Caroline
and your big brother, Liam*

*You are the seventh generation
of Connor in America.*

I

I came up with the title of this book on September 30, 2019, the day my father died. Dad had been on life support since September 20, when he'd had a heart attack in a rental car in a Costco parking lot in San Francisco, California, five minutes from the airport, to which he and Mom were about to drive to catch a plane home. I was supposed to pick them up at the Twin Cities International Airport. Mom had called me just after 3:00 p.m. as I bought a sandwich at the Jimmy John's on Grand Avenue in Saint Paul.

Mom and Dad had been sitting in that rental car, discussing their great four-day vacation, staying at the Marines' Memorial Club in San Francisco. They were talking about how much they loved each other, how much they loved their two sons and their daughter-in-law, Kellie (my brother David's wife), and their two grandchildren, Liam (15) and Caroline (13). They were talking about how lucky they were and how great a marriage they'd had for over fifty-one years and how they couldn't wait to get back home to the blessings of their family, friends, and life. Dad began pulling out of the parking spot and was struck with a heart attack, slumping over the wheel. Mom put the car in park and jumped out, yelling for help. Their Guardian Angels were watching over them.

There was a health fair going on at the Costco. Two EMTs responded, one of them utilizing a defibrillator, keeping Dad alive. Ten days later, shortly after 1:00 p.m. Pacific Time, which is 3:00 p.m., the hour of Divine Mercy, in our hometown of Saint Paul, I led Mom in the rosary, the Litany of the Blessed Virgin Mary, the canonization prayer for Blessed Solanus Casey, and the Chaplet of Divine Mercy over Dad in his hospital bed. He'd gotten his last rights three times in ten days, the last time around 9:30 that morning. That priest also gave him the Apostolic Pardon, reinstated by Pope Benedict XVI. Dad had his St. Christopher's medal around his neck, just as he had one Saturday morning when I, at age five, and David (6), encouraged by Mom's giddy smile behind her instructions, woke Dad up and climbed into bed with him to tell him it was time for breakfast. I remember being on his left side, David just beneath his shoulder and my face resting on the sheet covering his chest, just below his left pec, near his heart. David touched the chain around Dad's neck, pointing, saying, "Look, Mark—Dad wears that in case they find him dying somewhere."

"Really?" I said, "Like when he was in the Army?"

"Yeah," David said. "What do you call it, Dad?"

"This?" Dad said, pinching the medal between his thumb and forefinger. "That's my St. Christopher medal."

He held it off his chest so we could see then turned it around where there were words etched upon it.

"What's that say?" I asked.

"It says, 'I am a Catholic. Please call a priest.'"

David was really smart. He was pointing that medal out to me and asking Dad about it for my benefit. He wanted me to see that Dad had something around his neck to safeguard his religious practice, something that would remind others to facilitate his wish to be cared for and guided at the time of death by a priest. This was important to Dad, important to family, important in life. We were Catholic.

It's About Time is a phrase friends of mine often hear me say. Fighters I train, people I hang around with, and family members hear those words from me when they do something, no matter how significant or uneventful, oftentimes with a semi-irreverent tone. They say they'll be here soon, they bought a new car, they just got a job, or they're getting married. I reply, "It's about time!" The implication is we've been waiting forever, and you should've done this a long time ago, but it's also just me making light of the situation and voicing my approval, showing my support. Luckily for me, people are merciful enough to put up with my obnoxious personality, so I actually have friends. But it's about time, finally, I publish a book, as Dad knew too well.

The poems running through this story cover a lot of years, from the 1990s through 2019. Saint Paul poet, Danny Klecko, encouraged me in 2017 to put together a book. I started pulling out a bunch of stuff I'd written over the years, and Danny was going to help me get it launched, but he became absorbed in his own projects, including a collection—*Hitman-Baker-Casketmaker*—that won the Midwest Book Award, so our collaboration never materialized. You could say it got stuck in the snow, which is metaphorically accurate, given the night I premiered the first three poems of this book in the Clown Lounge downstairs at the Turf Club on University Avenue in Saint Paul, Wednesday, February 20, 2019. There were probably twenty people there that night because we'd had a blizzard that kept most people home. You couldn't blame them that year, one of the coldest and snowiest winters in our lifetime. But the crowd was good, and I owned the room. Here are the poems, along with the story wrapped around them.

The Perfect Metaphor
Monday, August 21, 2017 JMJ

The perfect metaphor to describe Boxing
        is jazz.
              There is a rhythm to every fight.

      I learned this from Dennis Presley
      who learned it from Rock White.

    A fighter has a rhythm
        and the only way to beat him
              is
            for you to break it
            and establish your own.
    That's where improvisation begins.
    No one knows where it will lead
    or where it will end.

Jazz is the perfect metaphor
        to describe Boxing.
        Every fight has its rhythm
        upon which is added improvisation.

I learned that from Dennis Presley
          who learned it from Rock White
          who practiced collaboration
          with Emmett Yanez and Bobby Zamora,
          the two men who taught me to fight.

Ever Since

Sunday, June 25, 2017 JMJ

Ever since our breakfast date
    I've been trying to come up
        with the perfect words to say,
  ones to make you stay,
        face to face with me,
        together.
     For two months or more
        I've tried to find the perfect phrase,
        whatever sets your heart ablaze,
        prompting your arms to wrap around me,
        the way they did when you found me
        arriving just a little late
        to our night of Irish music and our first embrace.

Oh, yes, I've tried and tried,
    and yes, I've even cried,
    knowing how I've made you frown,
    seen hidden pain in your quiet face,
    watched it ski
    a slalom race
    in between each girlish smile,
    me
    wishing you would trust this man,
    wishing you would take my hand,
    to let me lead you to a healing light.

Yes, I wish I knew
    exactly what to say to you,
    the words to tell to one who fell
    and wants to rise again.

    You are brilliant, you are beautiful,
    you are always—in my heart—my friend!

Yes, I wish I knew the perfect words to say.
    I know the perfect thing to do.
    I know, too, that you won't let me.

I must respect your freedom,
I must respect your privacy.

I want, I want, I try, I try
to find the perfect words to say or sing or cry,
but I just don't know them.

Apparently, God won't show them.

So I give up.

I give up effort.

But I don't give up desire, I don't give up hope, I don't give up patience, prayer, and love. I just give up effort. I give up all my words. And I give up you.

I give you up to God.

Two Pilgrim Souls, Anam Cara
Monday, September 11, 2017 JMJ

Over a century ago
    an epic poet
        from the land of our shared heritage
            wrote a poem
            to a woman,
                loving her soul's very pilgrimage.

His was a bitter poem,
            or so it seems,
                tempered by friendship's sweetness,
                      soothing his broken dreams.

It is true
    a man like me
        could feel the same for you,
        become Love run away,
        taunting your memory
                in your future, aged day.

But instead let it be said,
here on the ground
        and high among the stars,
this man loves the very monstrance you are.

And so,
    Anam Cara, Mo Chuisle, A Stóir Mo Chroí,
        remember:
            If you ever decide
                to be with me,
            one monstrance, too,
            we two will be.

I gave the whole spiel that Klecko suggested on stage, playing up my Boxer background, as well as the Irish American and Catholic identity. Dad grew up just a mile east of there, directly across the street from St. Columba, an Irish parish. Saint Paul is my city, even though I'm a product of a mixed marriage, Mom's family coming from Holy Rosary, over the border, in South Minneapolis. I enjoyed that night, feeling even more affirmed because Sabrina, a Mideastern graduate student I'd driven to the airport on a rideshare shift a week earlier, showed up with a girlfriend. They were both young and beautiful and alluring, as well as intelligent. Phil, a fighter and the manager at Element Gym, was there with his girlfriend, Ari, and we sat together in a booth. It was all passing though, fading the way life always does, so epic in the moment, so fleeting in time, so elusive in the now.

That poem, *Ever Since*, was written June 25, 2017 in a burst of energy that came over me in a fit of frustration. I'd been beating myself up over a mistake I'd made with a younger woman, thinking she'd cut herself off from me because of my intensity, my attempt to help her in a critical situation that was pivotal to her future, ultimately making matters worse. Later, which is to say a full three years later, I found out that she'd made a mistake I could have never helped her with and that I was lucky she was gone; my Guardian Angel was looking out for me. The ambivalence over romance with a younger woman is sometimes rooted in a fear of being perceived as an exploiter when, in certain situations, a man is the one in more danger of being exploited. But that poem broke a two-year writer's block, getting me back into a creative rhythm. I pulled Klecko out of the Boxing gym (he worked out at Element, where I was a private contract trainer and rented an office). We sat in my car, and I showed him that poem. That's when he said I had to get on stage, something I hadn't done in close to ten years. Circumstances as they were, it took almost two years to get there. Neither of the other two poems were even written yet.

Five nights after writing *Two Pilgrim Souls, Anam Cara*, on Saturday, September 16, 2017, I picked up Dennis McGrath, driving him to his son Dan's house to watch the rematch of Genady Golovkin against Saul Alvarez for the middleweight championship of the world on TV. Dennis was eighty years old by then and recovering from bladder cancer treatment. His wife, Betsy Buckley, nervously cautioned me on watching him as he walked, knowing he could get overconfident of his balance, which had been compromised by the cancer treatments that robbed a portion of his equilibrium and made his frame extra thin and frail. He'd been a mentor of sorts to me for the last ten years, after Fr. Kevin McDonough, the pastor of St. Peter Claver Catholic Church, the African American parish in Saint Paul, introduced us after Mass. Dennis was a graduate of the University of Minnesota School of Journalism and a Public Relations business legend in the Twin Cities. He'd been a partner in Mona, Meyer, McGrath and Gavin, which was bought by Weber Shandwick, one of the biggest firms in the world. He'd also graduated from DeLaSalle Catholic High School in Minneapolis, advocated for some of their basketball players who went on to play at the University of Minnesota, and contributed greatly to a journalism program that mentored young journalists of color at the University of St. Thomas in Saint Paul. When I met him, he was Communications Director for the Archdiocese of Saint Paul and Minneapolis, but he'd also been an Associated Press boxing writer early in his career. The first time I'd watched a fight at his house, he showed me the robe worn by Marvelous Marvin Hagler the night he lost the middleweight championship of the world to Sugar Ray Leonard. I can't remember if Marvin gave him that robe or how he acquired it, but it was a great piece of memorabilia. Dennis had also interviewed Rocky Marciano not long before a plane crash took Marciano's life, so he'd been around some legends of the sport. He loved the poem. It encouraged me. He was one of the people who kept me going.

Dennis knew exactly what the Irish words meant in English, and of course he knew what a monstrance is, too. 'Anam' means soul, and 'Cara' means friend, so 'Anam Cara' means 'Soul Friend.' 'Mo Cuisle' means 'My Pulse,' and 'A Stóir Mo Chroí' means 'Treasure of my heart.'

A monstrance is a gold plated cross with a round base so it can be stood on an altar, with a round, glass luna in the middle of the cross that opens and closes so a consecrated host, which is to say the body, blood, soul, and divinity of Jesus Christ, known by Catholics as the Blessed Sacrament, can be displayed in it.

At the time of the Turf Club performance, I was befriending a beautiful young lady who was a poet, painter, and photographer. She was tiny, mixed with African, German, and Mexican heritage, and had the prettiest head of dreadlocks I'd ever seen. She was twenty-six and recently out of a lesbian relationship, the only romantic relationship of her twenties, the only type of romantic relationship in her adult life. So, naturally, being a man, I had a crush on her. She didn't drive, and I knew she worked ten-hour days in Saint Paul and her light-rail commute between work and her Minneapolis apartment amounted to a twelve-hour day. I drove her home from work a couple of times a week to help her through that bitter winter. It was such a cold winter that one day the temperature, never mind the wind chill, dropped down to forty-two degrees below zero. I drove her knowing that nothing would happen between us, even though I wished it would.

Ironically, the first time I saw her, I couldn't stand her. I thought, she hates men. Then, one night while lying in bed, I thought, wait a minute, who am I to dismiss her? I'm supposed to be a Catholic, so I'm supposed to respect her, even if my view of life doesn't jive with hers. What if I just respect her? What if I treat her well and talk to her and let her know who I am? I'll bet, if I treat her respectfully, we're going to become friends. I'll bet she could use a friend, too. I know I could.

A couple of days after that poetry reading, we were driving to her building in Minneapolis, number 316, the same number as the hospice room in Saint Paul where my Uncle Tom died on February 12, a number that, through both associations, is permanently etched into my brain. Anyway, this beautiful woman with dreadlocks carried around with her a book she'd read three times, a text she used as a manual, a guidebook for her life, called *Women Who Run with the Wolves*. When she first offered to lend it to me, I said no, thinking I had no time to read something that long. It was written for women, I thought, and had to be super feminist and anti-man. But honestly, when she held it out to me, she was just so naturally alluring, as if taunting me, daring me to open my heart. I thought about her a lot. At the gym, I asked Ari if she'd read the book; she thought it sounded so interesting that she bought a copy for each of us. This beautiful, dreadlocked, tiny, charming, angry young woman knew I was reading the book, knew I respected her, had to know I had a crush on her, and she agreed we'd discuss this book when I finished. I'd fallen asleep while reading it late on Tuesday night, February 19 (the snowy night before the Turf Club performance), on my couch, musing, dreaming of my impossible little crush, waking up around 1:20 a.m., the wee morning hours of Wednesday, February 20. I immediately wrote this poem.

Halfway Around
Wednesday, February 20, 2019 JMJ

I'm halfway around to your way of thinking.
    All you have to do is come halfway around to mine
                  and we'll meet right here,
                              in the middle.

You convinced me,
        a Catholic man of Irish heart and old Saint Paul small town, big city tradition,
            to consider your alternative and read,
                Women Who Run With the Wolves.

Almost finished,
    I foresee
      our discussion
    leading to the reading
                of multiple books,
                  leading to mutually multiple pleasures
                  of a mental, physical, spiritual, and emotional nature,
                  peaking at the point of merger of difference and unity.

I foresee a building of our friendship
    in the building of our love,
        the building of family,
        the building of community.

Among like-minded we can build a pack,
    me the he-wolf to your she-wolf,
    embracing wild instinct
    guided by divine nature,
            living in finite wilderness
  civilized by infinite love.

I foresee me—
            facilitating you being the best you can be—
        sacrificing solitude for solidarity,
        finding freedom in obligation,
            my rest my responsibility,
            my commitment my liberation.

Later, on March 8, we were having a conversation in my car in front of her apartment building. We'd agreed on a coffeehouse date to talk about this book she so loved, *Women Who Run With the Wolves*, but we'd postponed it because of Uncle Tom's funeral. Now, she was cutting me off. She had all kinds of pressure on her from every direction in life and just wanted out. Not out of life, just out of any environmental pressure preventing her from developing her creativity, developing herself, developing the life she believed she was supposed to live. I personally saw any presence of me in her life to be a facilitation of her intentions, as *Halfway Around* explains. However, trying to keep the conversation going, knowing for her a copy of the poem was in the trunk of my car, I somehow could not articulate the need to give it to her. I knew, as soon as she walked out the door of my car, she wasn't communicating with me again. She was breaking ties with many, including me, believing she would rid herself of anyone who did not serve her purpose in life. She was leaving town.

I was heartbroken. After our final conversation, I felt literally that I'd been beaten up, though no one ever laid a hand on me. We were almost *Halfway Around* together, but now we were a world apart. On Sunday, March 31, waking up on my couch, I wrote the next poem, *Life So Simple*.

Life So Simple
Sunday, March 31, 2019 JMJ

As if to pray you start today in meditation on
    your bicycle wheel,
        the separate spokes united in the center.

You want me to be blunt, you say.
    I want to be direct
    but fear I'll frighten you away.

The final action is the original intention.
    This statement is authentically true,
        not just my invention.

My responsibility is to you
        a comfort for my rest,
        a respect in my behavior helping you to be your best.

You can push me away,
    invite me to stay,
    or walk with me today,
        but we met for a reason;
            to teach each other and learn.
            Such a fact comes not from acts,
            but is a grace we did not earn.

Demons distract, demons lie, and demons discourage us from our destiny
        till we die.

Friends encourage, friends assist, and friends persist
        with love on which we rely.

Your Guardian Angel already talked to mine.
Together they have watched us share laughter and argue to the point of crying.

You know they're sent by God, who really does exist
        and is not a tyrant or a terrorist.
            Rather, He is Love, Family, Life, held in common at the core—
            you and I specific spokes united in the center—
            spinning round from place to place
                and nothing more.

There were some other poems I put together qualifying for appropriate inclusion in this book. I've always held myself, of course, to the highest of standards, never believing any of these poems ready for an attempt at publication, so I never tried, which is why I so embarrassingly title the story, *It's About Time*. Dad challenged me once, as far back, I believe, as 2012, asking me why by the age of forty I hadn't published at least one book. If I really was a writer, as I asserted myself to be, I should have been able to publish at least five novels or other books by then.

        I told him to lay off,
        that there were legitimate reasons
              for current incompletion
              and that literary success was on its way,
                      but that was all an excuse.

The real reason was the lie
            in my heart
                that my work was going to be great,

                I just needed time to concentrate,

                which is always delayed right now for the job,
                or the friend in trouble
                      or another excuse,
                      which justified not trying.
                The truth is I was scared
                so I never dared.

If this book,
    which can fall flat on its face,
        is never presented to the public,
        I'll never know if you, the reader,
            recognize my talent.

If it does, in fact, fall flat on its face,
      at least metaphorically,
          I fall flat on mine.
      However, so what?

    It's about time.

II

Somewhere in between *Ever Since* and *Life So Simple*, I was immersed within *The Perfect Metaphor* on a daily basis, nursing nagging injuries that cut short professional boxing plans while secretly training for one last fight to go out on a win, sometimes quietly crying in the middle of my one thousand rep abdominal routine, other times joking with fighters and clients and trainers, doing straight job work to supplement my Literary Pugilism, and writing in my gym office, in my apartment, in cafés, or in city parks. I carried the voice of desolation in my heart countered by the hapless American expectation of perfection, staggered from the bluntness of my nation's cultural confusion, stabilized by the virtue of hope found in the priceless gift of faith, guided in mercy by angels. Here's a poem I wrote during that period, on a bench in Mears Park, Saint Paul, about three blocks away from the Catholic parish of St. Mark's. Along with *My Now Departed Brother*, it is my first literary publication, with a humble little publisher in Minnesota, Gabriel's Horn Press, in its first anthology, *Startled by Beauty*, 2019.

Upon the Finishing of My House Fried Rice

Upon the finishing of my House Fried Rice from
    Kim's Chinese restaurant
        while sitting on the bench by the tennis courts
            overlooking
            the baseball fields
                on Prior Avenue,
            enjoying the afternoon sun
                on my chest and legs,
                the Author of wisdom
                reached me
                    through a fortune
                      cookie.

    "You have a yearning for perfection."
'Tis a sharp observation,
    accurate and true,
    parentally harsh
        and merciful, too.
    Inwardly searching
        I easily see
        my old defection to an Empire of fear,
        one that ruled me
        in a spiral of failure
        till my childlike trust
        helped lead me here.

    My yearning for perfection
        I still hold dear.
        Yet with the press of this pen
            onto paper again
                I gratefully accept failure.
    After all, only the taking of
            another step
                gets me almost there,
                saving me from nowhere.
    Only humility protects me while here,
        defeating my arrogance.

    So with the press of this pen
        I try once again
        to end my poem here,
            knowing I know,
            however I know,
        we—
            children born in the Kingdom of Love—
            humbly outlive
                the empire of fear.

I wrote that poem in the summer of 2017, I believe. It's one of the few recent poems upon which I did not record the date. However, I remember clearly how hopeful I felt writing it. I was recognizing a certain sadness accompanying my life that is universal to all at some point, realizing that, in relationships and in personal endeavors, we often compromise our authentic selves without even being fully conscious of it. One mile northeast of the park bench on which I sat and wrote that poem was the Element Gym, containing my office, where I did much of my writing in between helping with the competitive boxing team and working with personal training clients. Before purchasing the House Fried Rice at Kim's on Marshall off Cleveland Avenue, I'd spent a little time kneeling in front of the Blessed Sacrament in the Adoration Chapel at St. Mark's. Dad was probably volunteering with the Military Order of the Purple Heart or else running errands or spending time with Mom at the family house on the far East Side, but his question of why I hadn't published any books yet was being addressed in my poem. It wasn't a straight answer given directly to Dad; rather, it was a clear answer addressed internally to myself. It was a boxer's answer, understood by the literary pugilist in his writer's heart.

My Now Departed Brother came to me on the night of October 8, 2018, as I mourned the death of David James Ruiz, a grade school friend of mine, who died roughly two weeks earlier, on September 26, from a motorcycle crash. I'd known him since third grade. He was the first black kid at St. Pascal Baylon Catholic Grade School. I saw him on the playground before school and thought, 'Hey, there's a black kid. That's pretty cool. I'll say hi.' But we weren't close back then. I went to junior high and high school at St. Thomas Academy, thirteen miles away in Mendota Heights. David transferred there our junior year from Johnson High. It was a rare East Sider who attended the Academy, so we got to know each other better. Then, after high school, we hung out quite a bit in our twenties. We drifted, though, both of us facing our respective challenges. The last I'd heard from him was a message he'd sent in January of 2018 on a Saturday afternoon. I was in my office at the gym, and he was telling me he'd written a play and asked how to protect the copyright. I sent a message saying he needed to register the copyright with the U.S. Copyright Office and I really wanted to talk to him but was too busy at the moment. I had too many things to do. The next time I heard anything about my friend was when I got a text message sent to me by our St. Thomas Academy classmate, Norb Winter, with poor David's obituary.

My Now Departed Brother
Monday, October 8, 2018 JMJ

So, "Oh, happy fall!" some people say,
   explaining away
      all confusion of God's plan,
         thinking man
            was destined to fall
               through God's active intention
                  for our behavior.

"Thank God
      that through the envy of the devil
         death entered the world,
         so Jesus Christ
         could become our Savior."

However, God always intended
         us to live lives that never ended
              in the Eden of Earth.

No, the sadness and pain
   of our fall
      actually came
      from selfish choices,
      but selfless revision
      ends our division,
      so we can rejoice.

'Tis impossible that He never intended
         to send Himself—
         through His Spoken Word—
         and yes, thank God
            for death!

After all,
    after our happy fall,
    we can return to unity
    with our Father,
    through His Son,
    in their Spirit.

But there is no reason to believe
> He did not in fact conceive
> a divine plan
> to speak Himself
>> into the incarnation
>>> of man,
>>> loving us so much
>>> that through His physical touch,
>>> even without our fall
>>>> we would see
>>>>> we are incarnate souls,
>>>>>> not each a soul
>>>>>>> trapped inside a body.

Oh, God bless you,
> my now departed brother,
>> best friend of all those years,
>> dead now from a motorcycle crash
>> and cause of all my tears!

You are gone from me—
> and Mom and Dad and family—
> but through all of our prayers
> and trust in Jesus' Divine Mercy,
>> through the grace of God
>>> we can be
>>> a communion of saints
>>> sharing in the beauty
>>> of all our prayers for each other,
>>> you remembering me
>>>> and me remembering you,
>> my brother in mutual memory of brother,
>>> always connected
>>>> to each other.

Here are a couple of poems I wrote while helping another departed friend, an eccentric old multi-millionaire, a personal training client, who died at age eighty in Reno, Nevada—first, *Ten Years Ago, by Buddy Guy*, which I wrote in 2016 in rural Nevada, where, carrying my gun, I'd driven him with hundreds of thousands of dollars-worth of gold he wanted to secure in a safety deposit box down there, then *Doing It Badly*, which I wrote in 2018 in Reno, Nevada when I was helping him through some major health issues. I wanted to develop fighters while training clientele willing to pay well, but since there was no money coming in from professional boxers at the time—a rare treasure with precarious preservable value—I occasionally worked quasi security detail, amounting to a combination of concierge service and genuine friendship that took long periods away from home. There were always suggestions of buying a gym I could run and managing professional fighters I could train, but between balancing a personal portfolio of multiple millions, lusting for women legally available in ways legally forbidden outside of Nevada, drinking way too much, and on rare occasions repentantly joining me for Mass as if he were turning over a brand-new leaf, my desolate friend was fighting demons of distraction, deception, and discouragement, forcing me to work his corner, and I, distracted from my own dreams, desperately telling him the strategies for spiritual survival, knowing I could only counsel from the corner, never able to enter the ring on his behalf, praying the angels could hold his fists up in front of his shoulders, protecting his chin from the fatal blows designed to destroy his soul. I tried to develop quality writing projects in my spare time, and these two poems will most likely become parts of much larger works.

Ten Years Ago, by Buddy Guy
CA November, 2016 JMJ

This song is haunting me,
    Ten Years Ago, by Buddy Guy.
This song is haunting me,
    Ten Years Ago, by Buddy Guy.
    Potentials from the past
    make me stop and wonder why.

This blues song haunts me,
    Ten Years Ago, by Buddy Guy.
This blues song haunts me,
    Ten Years Ago, by Buddy Guy.
    I could have gone this way
    and really went that,
        but right now is where it's at.

This song is haunting me,
    Ten Years Ago, by Buddy Guy.
This song is haunting me,
    Ten Years Ago, by Buddy Guy.
    Older men say I'm lucky,
    but I've made bad choices, I won't lie.

All I can do is keep on living,
    make the best of here and now.
All I can do is keep on living,
    make the best of here and now.
I thank God I finally know this,
    but Buddy, can you show me how?

Doing It Badly
Saturday, April 21, 2018 JMJ

Anything worth doing is worth doing badly,
        G.K. Chesterton would say.
   His most redeeming quality, as an Englishman,
        was his support for Irish freedom.
   His second most redeeming quality was his wisdom.
Anything worth doing is worth doing badly.

    So it was with you,
        even though what I decided to do
            drove you away.

    I have seemed a beast with a horn,
        just a losing warrior
            all battle torn,
                stumbling clumsily through emotional folly,
                not willing to admit the moment had passed
                and it was time to go home.

    You were another purpose for me,
        a budding young lady of beauty and need,
            rejecting my heart and the love I did bleed,
            clutching your pain as if it were greed,
            me standing, still, alone.

    Maybe I was supposed to just walk away,
            get to bed early, greet the new day.
            But something in your touch,
            something in your sigh,
            something in your smile
            behind your dark eyes
                    said you were worth it.

Yes, it is true, both for me and for you.

Anything worth doing is worth doing badly.

Doing it badly is a great concept from G. K. Chesterton. It is so true, anything worth doing is definitely worth doing badly. Think of how much God loves you. Okay, I understand we think so little of ourselves sometimes that we can't imagine people really loving us to the point of giving us everything, especially those whose relationships with their parents are really fractured. My heart grieves for those who don't have loving, sacrificing parents like I do. I understand, then, if you struggle believing the Creator of the universe loves you with that sacrificial love. He does, though, which is why it's so worthwhile loving Him. God gave you, the individual that you are, the sun you see in the morning and the moon at night. Whatever your troubles—be they a yearning for alcohol, a sexual selfishness, or anger and frustration—it's worthwhile to engage that battle for the love of God. You are so imperfect, like everyone else, that you will inevitably fail at loving God, but a perfect Father accepts a child's love at the child's capacity, not His own, so go ahead, love God badly; it's the only way you can.

III

Much of my writing is fueled by a practice I learned from a very good book about creative writing methods by poet Natalie Goldberg. Her book, *Writing Down the Bones*, suggests timed writing exercises. Many of these poems, if not all of them, are fueled at the root by this creative process, by this method. Unfortunately, or maybe fortunately, after using this method to compile a huge amount of writing when I left Saint Paul in May of 1994 and traveled to Seattle, Washington to get a salmon fishing boat job that took me into Southeast Alaska, I lost all the work the following year when it was stolen from my car. I'll get back to that story later, though. For now, I'll concentrate on recent poems. Also, let me say something about *Ten Years Ago, by Buddy Guy*. I really like that poem. I truly believe I'm saying something important about how quickly time flies and how precious life is, recognizing Buddy Guy's observation of the same reality in his song. A young black woman making her way in the music business, who worked with a poetry organization, came through the gym to learn to box. She was 26 years old. She came into my office and read some of my poetry, specifically *Ten Years Ago, by Buddy Guy* and *The Perfect Metaphor*. She didn't like *Ten Years Ago, by Buddy Guy* but really liked *The Perfect Metaphor*. I understand her attraction to that poem, but I was troubled by her inability to see the significance of my blues poem honoring a blues legend and his profound blues observation that is so universal in experience. The woman in question is very beautiful and very talented and would be easily identifiable in the Twin Cities music and arts community; she's popular. What is so poignant about my experience with, and understanding of, the poem *Ten Years Ago, by Buddy Guy* is that I first made the observation I am expressing, first understood the significance of Buddy Guy's song, at her age, twenty-six. Then, in my late forties, shortly before meeting her and sharing my poem with her, I actually wrote it. The dark, haunting observations in that song about the things the man would do if he could just go back ten years were so significant to me at age twenty-six, thinking how much better I could have made my life with one or two decisions at age sixteen, that the song has since stuck with me. My thought was, "Woman, you're only twenty-six; that's why you don't get the poem." But I got it at twenty-six, so why didn't she? Maybe it just wasn't for her. I concur, it's easy to argue *The Perfect Metaphor* is a better poem. I like them both for different reasons. But you can't deny *Ten Years Ago, by Buddy Guy* does its job, letting you know you have to "keep on living, make the best of here and now." I just wonder who can answer the question, "Buddy, can you show me how?"

The following poem I wrote on August 29, 2017. It was written about a time when I was still boxing, still thinking I'd be a national champion, still considering the possibility of fighting professionally. It's about a time when I was still innocent, relatively speaking. I was really in love then. Nothing ever seemed to work out, though, the way I thought it should. We were young Catholics rubbing up on the edge of right and wrong, close to indulging desires requiring commitments we were somewhat willing—and somewhat unwilling—to make, me thinking she'd see me in the picture of what should be, her not understanding how I failed to see where I just didn't fit. It's called *Irish Americans for Life*.

Irish Americans for Life
Tuesday, August 29, 2017 JMJ

I so wanted to make love with you in 1992,
    but I respected your purity
        to the best of my ability
        as we kissed a little longer,
        gripped each other—even stronger—
                              'till you said,
                                        'Stop.'

My poet friend, Tony,
        would have called you
                'a lightweight goddess with auburn hair.'

I so wanted to marry you,
        but you just didn't care,
            just wanted to go back home,
            didn't think I was good enough because I was not born over there,
                and anyway,
            I was not a member of the I.R.A.

My last date
    was with a girl
        one year younger than the daughter
                born to you and the ex-POW
                who absconded into alcohol and obscurity.

I've often thought
        how I could have caught
        a future with you
            if I would have pushed a little harder,
            learned how to barter
                my own integrity away,
            turning the night into our day,
                yielding a premature family.

You asked your dad's boyhood friend,
    Seamus Heaney,
    why I never followed through.

    'Because he's a true believer with a poet's heart,' he said to you;
            'Plus,
                he loves the Blessed Virgin Mary.'

That poem's title, *Irish Americans for Life*, is an amphiboly, like many of my titles. What's an amphiboly? It's a logical fallacy. It's a phrase that has more than one meaning. I like amphibolies for titles because they have a precision of meaning held simultaneously in multiple contexts. *Irish Americans for Life* could refer to being an Irish immigrant, who will now be American and have American citizens for descendants, it could mean Irish Americans dedicated to the Irish identity as an expression of their lives, or it could mean Irish Americans who are in fact pro-life. In this case, the Catholic identity is also central, although an Irish American identity could be protestant, like my buddy, Jimmy Galvin, who lived across the street from me in early childhood before he lost his dad to a heart attack and his mom moved them back to Eau Claire, Wisconsin, where she was from.

The speaker in *Irish Americans for Life* reminisces about a girlfriend in his youth whose father grew up with Seamus Heaney, the Nobel prize-winning poet from rural Derry, in the occupied six counties of Ireland. Heaney left his northern home for the Wicklow Mountains, journalists say, to get away from not just the English and their Loyalist paramilitary proxies but also the Irish Republican forces, who wanted him to represent the revolution. Upon his departure, a Belfast paper, representing the anti-Catholic, protestant, supremacist state of Northern Ireland, referred to Heaney as "a papist propagandist." Given the indisputable proof uncovered of British Empire collusion with Loyalist paramilitary death squads that murdered many Catholic civilians, it's not surprising Heaney would have received such public abuse from the press. Heaney had the audacity to write the truth, observing reality, gaining a high enough profile for his life to be threatened. Largely, it was because he was Catholic (and of course Protestants wanted to keep control of this last portion of Ireland physically occupied by England), but also because he was Irish and didn't identify as British. From 1968 to 1998, during The Troubles (as the Provisional Irish Republican Army war against British occupation of Ireland was named), Irish American identity grew in importance as a cultural revival, coinciding with the continuation of armed Irish rebellion. Dad didn't go around announcing Irish heritage to the world or expressing any opinion on the Irish question. Politically speaking, he was active with the Veterans of Foreign War (VFW), Disabled American Veterans (DAV), and Military Order of the Purple Heart. He'd been a first lieutenant platoon leader in the U.S. Army infantry and was wounded in combat in Vietnam. But he did join the Ancient Order of Hibernians (the oldest Irish Catholic fraternal organization in America) in 1985 and so did I in 1992. I always recognized in my heart a natural significance of Irish heritage and Catholic faith in my life as a resident of Saint Paul, but it wasn't until 2018, at a Division Four Hibernian meeting with my dad, that I realized, in a vividly articulable way, just how profoundly significant they are.

Dad grew up across the street from St. Columba Catholic church, a parish that was Irish. By Dad's time, everyone was already mixed, like Jeanne O'Gorman, the English teacher whom I assisted in the mid-1990s as her teacher's aide at Boy's Totem Town, a juvenile detention center in Saint Paul. Jeanne O'Gorman grew up a block or so from Dad, and although you can tell from her name that she's Irish, she's also part Italian. Even in the late 1800s, according to *Claiming the City: the power of faith and place in Saint Paul*, a book about Saint Paul by Mary Lethert Wingerd, the majority of Irish settling in Saint Paul were second and third generation, and those who were actual immigrants were, on average, brought by their parents to the U.S. and had lived in the country since early childhood. According to Wingerds' book, Saint Paul is the first city in the U.S. to have an Irish American middle class then, later, an Irish American wealthy class. So, naturally, St. Columba was an Irish parish, but Irish American as opposed to immediate Irish immigrant. Dad was an alter boy, and of course, that's when the Mass was celebrated in Latin, so he had to learn to speak that language as a young boy. He and his friend, Mike Byrne, were taught by Mike's dad, Bob Byrne. While Dad graduated from Bishop Cretin High School, Mike Byrne graduated from its rival, St. Thomas Academy. He also became a social studies teacher at the Academy's Middle School, and when it came time to start seventh grade, that's where Dad wanted us to go, through high school, starting with David, followed by me the next year, so I was taught Social Studies by Mike Byrne in seventh and eighth grade and was taught Latin by Bob Byrne in my freshman and sophomore years. I grew up seven or eight miles from Dad's childhood parish in the East Side parish of St. Pascal, went to junior and senior high school thirteen miles from there, but was taught by these two men from Dad's childhood. Then, one spring evening in 2018, sitting over a beer around a table after our Hibernian meeting in the old schoolhouse at Assumption Church on West 7th Street (one of the three active parishes remaining from the five originally operating out of downtown Saint Paul), Dad and I were talking with Bob McGarry, whose brother, Pat, was graduated by St. Thomas Academy with me. He said that his mom grew up in St. Columba parish also. Then, Hugh Kane, eighty-eight years old at the time (and still kicking at ninety as I write this book), sat next to me as I shared with Bob that Dad grew up in that parish.

"Your dad grew up in St. Columba?" Hugh asked me. We hadn't seen each other in a long time, and he momentarily didn't realize he knew me. I'd forgotten his name at the time, too.

"Yes, he did," I said.

"Who's your dad?

"He's right there," I said, pointing to Dad sitting on my right at the head of the table.

"And what's his name?"

"Bob Connor."

"And who are his parents?"

"Omer and Nell Connor."

"You're Omer and Nell's grandchild? Oh, I love them so much—they are the best neighbors I ever had!" he exclaimed.

It was an Irish conversation, really, Hugh not having been to a meeting in a while, not realizing he was sitting next to someone with whom he had a long-time connection, until the right word triggered his memory, reminding him he was among the truest of friends, the ones who are family.

Then, Bob McGarry told his story.

"My grandpa was an Irish immigrant, who became a manager at Montgomery Wards department store in New York," he said. "His boss told him, 'If you want to keep your job, you have to move to Chicago.' So, he moved my grandma, my mom, and her two sisters to Chicago. Then his boss told him, 'If you want to keep your job, you have to move to Saint Paul, Minnesota.' So, he came ahead to Saint Paul, and he was in the St. Columba parish looking for a place to rent. It was raining, and a milkman saw him. He asked what he was doing, and Grandpa said he was looking for a place to live for himself and his wife and kids. 'Get in,' the milkman told him, so he did, and the milkman took him to a fourplex for rent and introduced him to the landlord. He moved his family there, and so Mom grew up in St. Columba parish. Then, when my aunt was getting married, they had the groom's dinner at Mancini's. Grandpa goes to the groom's dinner, and after all these years, for the first time since that day, sees the milkman. 'What are you doing here?' he asks him. The milkman replies, 'My nephew's getting married.' The milkman's nephew was marrying my aunt."

That's Saint Paul for you, three generations of men—Hugh Kane, my dad, me, Bob McGarry (and his brothers Dave and Dan at the other end of the table)—all connected by one little parish, sitting in a Hibernian meeting at the church of the Assumption of Mary, talking about how everybody knew each other and everybody found a relative or a relative's friend, in the greatest overgrown small town never quite recognized for the big city it is.

Saint Paul is a big city, too, the Capital city, although it's smaller than most major cities, and both it and Minneapolis are more significant in conjunction with the other. We are a very literate metropolitan area and a very literate state, with many writers, the most famous of whom—and definitely my favorite—being F. Scott Fitzgerald, another Irish Catholic. During The Troubles, though, there was a solidarity built up with other communities and causes, particularly the American Indian cause. I remember a mural on Southeast 14th Avenue at Southeast University Avenue in Dinkytown, Minneapolis, the University of Minnesota neighborhood. I passed by that mural daily, between campus and my car, my last year and a half of college. It was on a wooden newsstand run by a man named Indra, an immigrant from India. He allowed Bob Kelly, an Irish American who worked at Heart of the Earth Survival School—a culturally specific, alternative Charter school in Dinkytown partially founded by Ojibwe Psychologist and playwright, Chuck Robertson—to put together two paintings on the newsstand with his students. One painting, facing University Avenue, was a huge portrait of American political prisoner, Leonard Peltier, the American Indian Movement (AIM) member in Leavenworth Federal Prison for life. Two FBI agents were killed when AIM fought back in a standoff on the Pine Ridge Reservation in South Dakota in 1972. Peltier's trial was a farce, and although he says he knows who killed the agents, he won't name names, so he remains in prison. The side of the newsstand facing 14th Avenue was painted with a circle of the faces of the ten men who died in the 1981 Irish Hunger Strike. In the four corners of the mural were the symbols of the four provinces—Connaught, Ulster, Leinster, and Munster—of Ireland. The Hunger Strikers who died between May 5 and August 20, 1981 are Bobby Sands, Francis Hughes, Ray McCreesh, Patsy O'Hara, Joe McDonnell, Martin Hurson, Kevin Lynch, Kieran Doherty, Thomas McElwee, and Mickey Divine. Eight of them were members of the Provisional IRA, and Patsy O'Hara and Mickey Divine were members of the Irish National Liberation Army (INLA). Obviously, each of these men were engaged in a vicious, bloody war and were willing to kill and die for the cause of Irish freedom to unite their country. Peltier stands for a different kind of national sovereignty, a self-determination of indigenous nations, who signed treaties with the U.S. government and are citizens. Cultural survival and maintenance of indigenous language, for the tribes here and for the people in Ireland, are also large parts of the battle.

 The following poem, *Little Belfast Sister*, I wrote in 1997 shortly after Nationalist riots broke out over the Loyal Orange Order being pushed through the Catholic Garvaghy Road community in Portadown, County Armagh. The Orange Order is a pro-British, anti-Catholic, Protestant fraternal organization celebrating and perpetuating British rule in Ireland. Portadown, where the Orange Order was founded in 1795, is a town of a little more than 20,000 people that is roughly seventy percent protestant and thirty percent Catholic, the majority of the latter living in the Garvaghy Road community in housing estates, or projects, as we'd call them in America. Roughly fifteen hundred British troops, the Royal Ulster Constabulary military police force, a Loyalist paramilitary presence and up to fifty thousand Unionist,

Loyalist supporters regularly escorted the Orange Order down the Garvaghy Road every summer to remind the Irish Catholic community they were still colonized. In writing the poem, I remembered a call I'd made the previous Christmas to a friend in Belfast I'd met when he'd come over to Saint Paul as a chaperone for the Irish Political Prisoners Childrens' Holiday Program. The children of prisoners were brought to various states, such as New York, New Jersey, Pennsylvania, Massachusetts, California, Minnesota, and Illinois, to stay with sponsor families from June through the end of July, the time of year when the largest number of anti-Catholic parades celebrating British rule would force themselves through their communities. (The Marching Season actually lasts from the day after Easter into September.) In the fall of 1996, I'd stayed with my friend a few days at his parent's house in a Nationalist enclave in Loyalist controlled North Belfast, roughly six months after the first prolonged IRA ceasefire had ended. He showed me around, took me to the GAA (Gaelic Athletic Association) for drinks, and we attended the premiere showing of the movie, *Michael Collins*. I called the week after Christmas, 1996, and when he answered, I asked how he was doing.

"Not too well," he said. "My friend just got his legs mangled in a car bomb."

"Really?" I said.

"Yeah, the Loyalists broke their ceasefire."

The next summer, 1997, I spoke with Kate Conlan—Chuck Robertson's wife and the Minnesota coordinator for the Irish Political Prisoners Childrens' Holiday Program—and wrote an article for a local alternative paper about the issue. I thought about the war over there and the trouble people were going through, and I remembered two things: one, the phone call I'd made a couple of days after the last Christmas and, two, a little girl I'd seen while I was walking down the Falls Road in Belfast that fall, heading back towards my friend's house. I'd been taking pictures of the murals and saw this blond-haired little girl, roughly seven years old, in her Catholic girl's school uniform, carrying her school bag while walking home. Passing a Hunger Striker mural on her right, she stopped, still facing forward, pumped out a quick set of Irish stepdance moves, then walked on. Wow, I thought, that was so beautiful. It's still my favorite memory of Belfast. So, thinking of the current situation and remembering her, I wrote this poem, *Little Belfast Sister*.

Little Belfast Sister

July, 1997   JMJ

Little Belfast Sister
with the seven-year-old locks of golden hair,
    I wonder how you are over there,
        wonder if you still stepdance past Hunger Striker mural.

Thought of you on Christmas Eve
        when Loyalists broke supposed ceasefire
        with car bomb mangling of young man legs,
        think of you now
        when Orange Order march explodes
                      bomb
                      of Irish anger defending your youth,
                      protecting your gift of step dance moves
                      with hijack of Dublin-Belfast commuter train
                      and buses and cars to be burned for blockade
                      against British brigades
                      of storm trooping goosesteps,
                      gasoline bomb guerillas pelting tanks with
                      fire of freedom,
                      Orange Halls incinerated
                      after last straw of Portadown
                      bringing slave master's aggression tumbling down.

        First time I've seen July 12 somehow bring
    promise with my birthday,
            whispering
                fantasies of Belfast—
                                still same as Pine Ridge—
                                only this time, healing.

How long a divide and conquer carnage need be
    before building bridge of United Irishman bicentennial
    destroying sectarian ignorance for true rebellion against invader?

Will Loyalists learn to join Irish Republican Presbyterian truth
     for fight in name of common Celtic roots,
    or must brainwash persist to keep hearts turned traitor?
    And in midst of all this I still see you,
                  golden-locked little Irish hearted sister,
                  dancing still off the Falls Road
                                  across Hunger Striker mural.

My angry fanatic heart still feels pain of ever still higher climbing flames,
            you still dancing
                with precious boxes of sevens and circles of threes,
                continuously touching the deepest crying soul of me,
                triumphantly moving across Hunger Striker Mural.

Red Brother coming soon, Red Brother running soon
sacred prayer across your land for you.
Must be pure power prayer make killers go home,
finally leave families alone,
you—my purest triumphant sister—step dancing past Hunger Striker Mural.
                            Still stepdancing past Hunger Striker Mural.

Rereading that poem, included in *Stand Off On The Irish Road,* a never produced play I wrote about the Garvaghy Road, I'm startled at the emotions in it, remembering how deeply I felt them at the time of its writing. The reference I make to "building bridge of United Irishman bicentennial truth/ destroying sectarian ignorance" alludes to the United Irishman Rebellion of 1798, which was led by a Presbyterian, Theobald Wolfe Tone, uniting Catholic, Protestant, and Dissenter. After that rebellion was defeated, the Loyal Orange Order, which was founded three years earlier in 1795 only for Anglicans of the upper class, opened membership to other Protestants, wedging a divide between Catholics and Protestants over the next two hundred years. One lyrical influence in the poem was music from Black 47, an Irish folk-rock band led by Irish immigrant Larry Kirwan. On their 1992 album, they have a song called *My Fanatic Heart* about the Orange marches. Another influence is the late poet John Trudell, the former spokesman for AIM. Poor John lost his wife and children, as the story goes, to a mysterious fire when he wasn't home, not long after he'd been told—warned by an FBI agent—that his bold public statements for American Indian rights were dangerous, were the kind of statements that get people killed. I used to listen on an old Walkman with headphones to a cassette tape of his poetry and Irish Rebel songs, including *Fire of Freedom* by Black 47, on the flipside, while working overnight at Aín Dah Yung (Our Home) Center, a temporary emergency homeless shelter for American Indian youth. This Irish friend of mine, the firstborn American of his family, made that tape for me. In September 2003, I believe, when John was in Saint Paul for a Labor Day celebration on Harriet Island on the West Side Flats off of downtown, I was driving taxi and sitting at a cab stand across the river in front of the Saint Paul Hotel. I watched him walk out of the hotel and into Rice Park, then not long later, I saw him returning towards the hotel, so I got out of the cab and approached him.

"Excuse me—John Trudell?" I said.

"Yes," he said.

"Hi. My name's Mark Connor," I explained, holding my hand out to him, "and I just wanted to say, I really appreciate your work. I'm a writer, and I'm driving cab right now, and I work at a homeless shelter for American Indian kids. I want you to know I really appreciate what you do."

"Well thank you," he smiled. "Thank you for what you do."

I didn't ask for his autograph, and I didn't try to connect with him professionally, and I didn't ask him to read my writing or help me get published. I just expressed my appreciation, and he expressed his back to me with a grand smile. We blessed each other and wished each other good luck, and he went back into the hotel. A day earlier, I had met philosopher and political activist Cornell West on Harriet

Island at that Labor Day celebration, and he thanked me for what I do and encouraged me to continue doing it. At this point in my life, it's obvious that West and I passionately disagree on many social moral issues, but I find his friendship with his colleague, Princeton Law Professor and Catholic civil rights advocate, Robert George, to be the kind of example of the respect and national solidarity I hope we can return to in our country, presuming it has—at least at points of temporary synchronicity—existed before. *Little Belfast Sister* signifies the love that holds people together, rooted in family, held in common across cultures, flaring in anger when pressured over time while restricted by the suffocating confines of conquest. Similarity in suffering yields understanding and sympathy, so AIM members who practiced the Sacred Runs, which are religiously ceremonial relay runs across large masses of land, praying for peace and justice, came to Ireland for a sacred run at that time. That was the reference I made to "Red brother coming soon . . ." in the poem. I read that poem in front of a crowd in Dublin once in 1998, but a few weeks before that, I recited a different one instead because a man I worked with, who was from a Unionist area outside Belfast, was present, and I didn't want to cause hostility. I also got the chance to place it in the hand of Bernadette Sands McKevitt, little sister of Bobby Sands and a founding member of the 32 County Sovereignty Committee, at Cumann na Moentoir (the Teacher's Club) in Dublin after she spoke against the Good Friday Agreement. I have read it in Saint Paul and Minneapolis in public, once at Kiearan's Irish Pub in Minneapolis, getting mixed reactions. At Kieran's, most of the small crowd seemed receptive to it, but the hostess of the open mic mocked it, confirming the range of reaction to be expected of such a poem. My poetry has been more well received at the Dubliner in Saint Paul.

I'd written a bunch of freelance articles for various publications and, in the late 1990s and early 2000s, published a lot of them in an alternative Twin Cities weekly in Minneapolis. I was Assistant Managing Editor of the paper from January to June 2001, until the crazy Maoist owner (that's right, repulsive as it is, the man is a Maoist) decided I was not docile enough to his ideology, so he replaced me. I'd been one of five different editors that year, which tells how difficult the man was to work for, although the atmosphere maintained by the other employees made it enjoyable. I didn't feel up to sending out my résumé to seek journalism work at the time, so instead I decided I'd drive taxi for three months. That quickly turned into three years (explaining why I was outside the Saint Paul Hotel when John Trudell was there). I was driving around, making very little money one frustrating afternoon in February 2003, when I called the shelter Aín Dah Yung, where I was still officially listed as an on-call employee. Lynn, my former coworker who'd become the current manager, answered. I asked if she needed extra help, and she needed it desperately, so I started working the overnight shift on-call, becoming the permanent weekend overnight employee within a year. I worked that job, drove cab the 12-hour dayshift a couple of times a week (including on Fridays before going to the shelter), ran my personal training business, Fighting Chance/Boxing for Life, Monday through Thursday, sought freelance writing assignments and worked on a novel. I couldn't have possibly been overextending myself, could I?

Constantly tired, always worried that I wasn't writing enough or wasn't at the gym enough, frustrated that I wasn't pulling in enough money on my freelance endeavors to quit my straight job, I was at that shelter every Friday, Saturday, and Sunday at 11:00 p.m., working till 8:00 a.m. the next morning. One night, at least a year into that overnight position, there was a little black boy—five years old and placed in shelter just that day—who slept on the couch because he was too scared to be on the boys' floor in the darkness of the old house, and while I was in the kitchen doing the dishes after midnight, I heard him crying hysterically through the sound of the water spraying on pots and pans. I remember there was nothing I could do, so I just kneeled on the floor next to the couch and gave him a hug and rocked back and forth, saying, "You're a good boy; you're a good boy."

At the time, on Monday mornings, Dad would pick me up at my apartment after work and take me to breakfast. I'd been doing so many things, reaching the middle of my thirties and trying to establish myself to the level I thought I should have reached in my twenties, so I was very busy. Dad told me he wasn't spending enough time with me in my adult years and wanted me to commit to seeing him once a week. That was a time when Dad altered his approach to many issues in life, even, eventually, at Mom's insistence, going to counseling at the V.A. and getting evaluated for post-traumatic stress disorder. Even though he'd been married his entire adult life, had no chemical dependencies, and was never unemployed, which were considered the biggest indicators at least on the surface level, he said, they diagnosed him with it. That's understandable because he saw a lot of fighting and death in Vietnam and almost died there before his twenty-fourth birthday. But I told him he was crazy; there was no way I could commit to seeing him once a week. I just didn't have the time.

"Why not?"

"Because, Dad, I'm trying to do so many things. I just don't have the time."

"Fine," he said. "I guess you can come spend time with me at my funeral."

That hit me hard. I committed to his request, and we had breakfast together once a week for the last fifteen years of his life. That's the best decision I ever made. Anyway, he picked me up Monday morning after the weekend I'd worked when I had to comfort that five-year-old boy alone at the shelter. He said "Hi," and we sat for a moment as I told him about it, and I just couldn't help it—I started to cry a little. It was good to be with my dad. I always knew who he was and that he was always in my life and I was always his son. I never had any confusion about who I was or to whose family I belonged. Later that year, when I met with Lynn in her office for my employee evaluation, she gave me a great compliment.

"The way I see you," she said, "is you're like the doorman."

"Really?" I said.

"Yeah, you know like the doorman in the sweat?"

"Yeah," I said, "I know exactly what you mean."

The doorman is positioned by the door in the sweat lodge, ready to yell out, "Ahao, Mitakuye Oyusin!" (which means "All my relations" in Lakota and Dakota) signaling the fireman, standing outside, to pull open the cloth door to let air in and cool it down. The doorman makes sure everyone in the sweat lodge is physically all right, that no one gets hurt from the intense heat.

"Yeah," she said, "especially for the younger kids. Your role here is to make them safe." Sometime in the next year or two, being both lonely and alone, realizing I was in the latter portion of my middle thirties, still hadn't found a wife, and still spent all my weekends (the time I believed people were out meeting the ones they'd be with), working awake overnight in that shelter, I wrote the following poem, *They Call Me a Doorman*. It's actually a false start, the opening to a much longer story I never got back to, but it came from that conversation with Lynn, so I include it here as a short, stand-alone poem.

They Call Me a Doorman
CA 2005 JMJ

They call me a doorman.
That's because I watch the door.
    I guard the door.
    I protect the people.
    I didn't choose this role; it chose me.
    The people decided, and I accepted.

I guess I didn't really have a choice,
    unless I wanted to spend my days in hell,
    because that's the price you pay
        when you refuse your destiny,
        or so I have learned,
        but that is my personal
        understanding of the human journey
        through life,
        and it is better explained
            at a later time.

Suffice it for now to say I am a doorman.
    Stay with me through my story and,
        if you hear with your heart
        as well as you can listen
        with your ears,
        when you are ready
        you will understand.

Lynn had spent time in her teenage years going to sweat lodge and other Dakota ceremonies with a circle of people—a Hochoka, or spiritual family—on the Prairie Island Dakota reservation roughly thirty-eight miles south of Saint Paul. The Prairie Island Sweat, at the Black Horse Camp, is a sobriety sweat started by Amos Owen in the 1980s. Participants were asked to be sober four days prior to the sweat lodge and four days after. If they kept to that commitment and attended every week, they'd stay sober. Even though I've never had a compulsion to drink, I hadn't had a drink since a year before starting work at Aín Dah Yung in 1995, and I didn't smoke marijuana because I believed that the kids would see it in me, so being sober—a requirement for serious travel on the Red Road—wasn't a problem. An Irish American poet, Kevin O'Rourke, took me out there in 1997, and when I returned from six months in Ireland in 1998, Darwin Strong, husband of Gabby Strong, the Executive Director of Aín Dah Yung when I first worked there, attended sweat lodges with me at Prairie Island and took me with the leaders of that Hochoka, Art Owen and his little brother, Ray Owen, to the Sundance ceremony in Kyle, South Dakota on the Pine Ridge reservation in August. I went there each year from 1999 through 2003. Art, a United States Army hand-to-hand combat veteran of the Vietnam War, died roughly a year before Dad did, in October 2018. Unfortunately, I was in New York when it happened, so I missed the funeral. A character in my (still never produced) play, *Stand Off On the Irish Road*, is based on those two men, mostly on Art, God rest his soul, but significantly on Ray, too. I was working regular weekend overnights at Aín Dah Yung by then, so I was unable to attend the Friday night sweat lodges on Prairie Island because they didn't begin till well after 8:00 p.m. and ended too late for me to make the 11:00 p.m. start of my shift. Also, I didn't feel I could responsibly attend Sundance that year because I couldn't afford to skip work. I'd just started my personal training business, Fighting Chance/Boxing for Life, a year earlier, had returned to pursuing freelance writing assignments seriously, was attempting a final revision on my first novel, was driving taxi part-time, and was trying to get back in shape. Although I originally still attended Sunday Mass in addition to going to sweat lodge on Friday nights, I began to skip the Mass occasionally, making it no more than once a month at that point. Realizing how important the weekly religious observance was, I returned to Mass every Sunday. It was difficult, too, because I either stayed up after work on Sunday morning or got up early Saturday afternoon for the 4:00 p.m. vigil (which counts as the early Sunday Mass) at St. Peter Claver while fatigued by the night shift hours. That's when I started my return to full observance of the Catholic faith. A few years later, a gorgeous girl I was in love with from Colombia asked me what brought me back. It was the Blessed Sacrament, I told her. I couldn't believe she didn't understand the necessity of the Blessed Sacrament or that she was deciding to abandon it herself.

Before sharing the next poem, there is a point I must make about Indigenous Americans and my involvement with them in order to be honest and respectful. When I mention the sweat lodge and the Sundance Ceremony, it is important to explain that I am not a Sundancer and am not an authority on American Indian spiritual tradition. I know a lot more than the average person and am close to people within the community, but I am not American Indian, and I don't pretend to have grown up with these traditions. Darwin Strong always respected me, and I believe he recognized a true respect for and desire to learn from American Indian people within me. He invited me to learn more, and we grew in friendship. My knowledge is mostly based in Lakota or Dakota tradition, and the Sundance ceremonies I attended were on the South Dakota Rosebud reservation in the mid-1990s and the Pine Ridge reservation between 1999 and 2003. Darwin, as the husband of Gabby, a Medwaketan Dakota, went with Gabby to Kyle where she attended Sundance, and that's where he became a Sundancer. When he took me there with Art and Ray Owen and those who traveled with them, he was taking me as part of the Helper's Camp. Art, Ray, and Darwin were all Sundance warriors who helped the Sundance Chief to lead the ceremony, which, after four days of preparation, lasts four days and consists of singing and dancing around a cottonwood tree from sunup to sundown in prayer to God—the Creator, called 'Thunkasila Wakan Tanka,' or 'Grandfather, Great Mystery' in the Lakota language—for another year of life for the people. There are medicine men, who are called Haokas, which are sacred clowns, who are allowed to conduct ceremonies backwards (physically moving counterclockwise instead of clockwise) on occasion. Darwin never had a full vision to be a Haoka, but he is considered halfway in between a regular Sundancer and a Haoka. He is actually from the Ojibwe tribe on the Red Lake reservation in Northern Minnesota, but because he went with Gabby to Pine Ridge (and because he's also part Lakota on his mother's side), his Sundance commitment is through the Lakota Nation. I have great respect for this tradition. I find, in particular, the belief that during a sweat lodge ceremony the ancestors come into the sweat lodge, dance on the heated rocks at the center of the sweat lodge, hear the people's prayers, then carry them to the Creator, is parallel to the Catholic belief in the Communion of Saints. As Auxiliary Bishop of Los Angeles, Fr. Robert Barron said, the Catholic approach is to recognize the truth where it exists, find how we have it in common with other cultures, and point from it to where it coincides with our understanding of the totality of truth. Herein I see where the differences between me and American Indians merge at a point of unity. At Sundance, as part of the Helper's Camp, my job was to make sure, along with the other family and friends who were with us, that Darwin and Art and Ray were okay, so they could help continue the prayer of the Sundance ceremony for the people. The young warriors were making their physical, dancing prayer while fasting sunup to sundown from food and water under the hot sun. The helpers assisting the Sundance Chief had to be hydrated and had to eat well at night in order to watch over and assist these young warriors. I always felt refreshed, renewed, reinvigorated, and full of hope upon returning from the Sundance ceremony.

Now, since I say I came home full of hope from the Sundance ceremony, let me share a poem I wrote around September, 2004. It's a hopeful poem written when I was full of that overnight shift fatigue.

An Hour of Ambivalence

CA September, 2004 JMJ

Even though it felt like an hour of ambivalence,
    it was wonderful.
      With everything up to that point, and even now,
        left unresolved,
          I feel the priceless gift in each moment that evolves.

In love with pretty, enamored with gorgeous,
   and knowing you to be an expression of the whole,
         I adore beauty in her totality.

A combination of excitement and fatigue,
      indifference and anticipation,
        a cup of coffee at the corner table by the picture windows
       with a view of the crossroads intersection of the
       gray afternoon, just before the fall of night,
       there it is—we two, swimming, fully clothed
       in the muddy waters of a smoky coffeehouse—
        sharing the mutually exposed nudity of our individual
                   souls.

Questions of origin and destination, arrivals at age and levels of maturation,
    in the absence of lust
      our precarious agreement emerges in the secure vulnerability of
                  trust.

Strolling up the block and around the corner,
a glimpse at the tops of the trees reveals them already bare,
            perfect and precious as your warm neck,
            exposed by your loosened red scarf
            and touched by your soft black hair.

Sitting in your car, parallel parked in a bed of crunchy leaves,
    you smiled up at me
        in acceptance of a wish for a wonderful eve.
   To your wish of the same I tuned back to say
            it was already guaranteed.

Walking away and into the night, and the brilliance of many more before
                  resting in sleep,
   I was wearing—and wallowing in—your wonderful smile,
   the one that forever in my heart I will keep.

I like that one, too. It's just a recognition of a gift, an observation of a pleasant experience that I'll never forget. Hopeful, always hopeful. I was in my mid-thirties, had skipped going to the Sundance that summer but was still working at the shelter for American Indian kids, where I would be employed another five years. And I was altering my journey just a little, still burning sage each night once the kids were all in bed at the shelter, smudging off each room and praying for each child before starting my shift of doing their laundry, doing leftover dishes and cleaning the kitchen, cleaning the bathrooms, cleaning and straightening the living room, looking in each bedroom on the hour to make sure every kid was there, and hopefully sitting at the desk to write. That's what my Bachelor's of Arts degree in English was for, to help me be a better writer; it might have made me a better youth care worker, too, but being a youth care worker also helped me to write, even when it seemed to be more an enemy than a friend to the literary life.

I really solidified my connections in the writing and boxing worlds between 2009 and 2016 as a Trustee on the National Executive Committee of the National Writers Union (UAW Local 1981), when I used to make two trips a year to our headquarters in New York to perform semi-annual audits with one or both of the other Trustees, but I'd been traveling to the city since 1996, and the only friend I stayed with was Nick Bryant, who moved there from Minneapolis in 1995 and has made his living as a freelance journalist ever since. From 2004 through 2007, I made a trip each early December to see him. He's been published in some big magazines, and he's now interviewed on widely circulated podcasts because he wrote *The Franklin Scandal*, in which he mentions me in the acknowledgements because I gave him friendship and support during that project. Suffice it to say, my friend Nick has gone through a lot of strife and come out stronger for it. Because he uncovered a network of child trafficking, Nick is recognized as somewhat of an expert on the issue, and although he's not the only one who covered the story of Jeffrey Epstein, he is the one who put Epstein's black book on the internet.

An Hour of Ambivalence was written a year before social media became a trend, even before smoking was banned in restaurants and bars. Things really changed overnight, or so it seems. As I said, I was altering my journey just a little. While working in the Native American Indian community, I was drawn to the deeply religious approach to life. I'm often told the Red Road is spirituality, not religion, but that's not true. It really is religion because the traditional beliefs don't change, there are structured rituals, and it's based on how God made us—that's a conversation for another time, though. As my journey altered, I just began embracing more of who I am, returning more to my Catholic faith while maintaining my love and respect for the Red Road. Between 2003 and 2005, while home alone trying to find the right balance of rest and wakefulness in relation to my third shift and daytime portions of the week, I occasionally watched a segment on Eternal Word Television Network (EWTN), which I'd first seen when my parents watched it once or twice before I moved out of the house. I also occasionally tuned into a radio channel I'd accidentally discovered in my car, 1330AM, Relevant Radio, a Catholic radio station. (The first couple of years, I rolled up the windows or turned the radio down on a corner or near a person who knew me, though, embarrassed to be discovered listening to Catholic radio.) By 2007, still holding a rebellious, alternative leaning spirit in my heart, I decided to start praying the rosary. This was all triggered by my working at Aín Dah Yung again, which kept me from regularly attending the Prairie Island Sweat (or Aín Dah Yung sweats), given that I was either sleeping or working when they happened. It led me to deciding I had to stop any tendency toward casual relationships with women; I had to return to my childhood religion if I was ever going to get married and have kids.

"Marriage is overrated," Dad told me in one of our breakfast conversations.

"Really?" I said. "But you've been married all these years to Mom; do you regret it?"

"No," he said. I wish I could quote his exact words, but I didn't retain them. He said their similarity in education and mutual faith were critical to them being together. He was trying to alleviate my anxiety, though, of not having found someone at that point in life.

"Let's just say, some people marry for the sake of the institution," he said. "That doesn't mean they're right for each other. Don't marry someone just to get married. Do it if that's your vocation."

It has to be your calling in life, he told me, specifically with her.

Fully returning to the faith, following the rules, I thought I might get to that point. Hopeful as I was when writing *An Hour of Ambivalence*, it's ironic that, thirteen years later, I was still alone, still had no kids, and I wrote something like the following poem about writing the perfect poem.

43

I Was About to Write the Perfect Poem
Tuesday, November 7, 2017 JMJ

I was about to write the perfect poem;
        had it all in my head
                when I got home.

      I took a shower first, instead,
          mouthing the words
                  directly to you,
        the way I always seem to do
                  when you're not here.

I mouth my words to my buddies, too,
              explaining what is perfectly clear,
            subtly blunting the obvious truth.

They're not here; you're not here.

      I am just alone.

      Being alone for too long
          can definitely make you crazy.

Here I am, talking to you,
      while I'm alone.

I was about to write the perfect poem.

    That's right, I was about to do it. Obviously, there was no other line to write after that one. I guess the next task was to write, once again, the imperfect poem.

IV

The imperfect poem. As far as I'm concerned, I was writing some pretty good stuff from the summer of 2017 through the fall of 2019. Looking back at it now, of course, I find it all imperfect, but I feel much more comfortable with some of them than I did back then. The following one keeps my mood of the time, a mood Dad noticed and worried about, one of sadness. One thing I assured him of, though, was it was not despair.

"But, Mark—" Dad said to me in front of Mom in the living room before I left the house one Sunday, after we'd been out for breakfast, "… you're so sad all the time. It worries me because I know you have guns."

"Oh, no, Dad," I said, "you never have to worry about that, because I believe in the Blessed Sacrament. No matter how sad I get or how depressed I am, I go sit in that Adoration Chapel in front of the Blessed Sacrament, and I'm okay."

He had no answer to that. He was frustrated. I wasn't doing anything bad. I was just going through a challenging time, when things weren't working out, while it always seemed I was on the edge of some major opportunity that never quite materialized.

The following Friday, I reassured Mom. She reassured me. She visited me in my apartment. I am a combination of them, a one flesh union, an expression of their love. Men are hard. Some things you just don't tell Dad, but you might tell Mom. I showed her some of these poems. She understood the most important lines, like, "I must respect your freedom, I must respect your privacy."

My sadness was not of despair. No, as cynical as I sometimes seem, I hope others can see hope within me. I never lose hope.

Knowing You
October 23, 2017 JMJ

Knowing you has been the hardest challenge
                of my life,
        even harder
              than living 48 years
                      and never having a wife.

    I foresee a time
        when you finally will come back around,
                full circle
                    to me.

    I hate the waiting,
                in spite of attention
                      from other women
                              whose pleasant voices and gentle presence
                          comfort me.

But your fickle female nature,
            coupled with the softness of my heart,
                    prompted you,
                          for now,
                              to depart.

It's all private,
        not meant for the page,
        not meant to be read by others,
        not recited before crowds
                of judging women
                    and disrespectful men,
            or even flow from
                the ink of the pen.

I knew from the start
　the storm you could be
　　　　　　　and often are.

I do not believe the world owes me any sympathy.

　　　Someone once said,
　　　　　　　"Until a man knows he's a man,
　　　　　　　he will be trying to prove he is one."

I say,
　until a woman knows she really is a woman,
　　　　　　she won't demand a real man
　　　　　　　　　　because she can't even see one.

The first year of my return to regular work at Aín Dah Yung (2001 was the only year I remember not doing at least one on-call shift), I slowly saved enough to quit the taxi driving gig. Then I started running more and getting to the boxing gym regularly again, getting back in shape. Dad thought that was cool. He loved the fact that I could keep my physical condition into my later thirties, dealing himself with physical limitations caused by shrapnel in his legs and a shattered kneecap from Vietnam. He also hoped I'd make decent money personally training people irrespective of whether I trained competitive fighters. I, of course, in my egomania, started desiring to enter the ring again. My original thought wasn't to fight, though, just to spar with the professionals getting ready for their fights, because I did that with Will Grigsby, my teammate from the Inner City Youth League, who'd gone to the National Golden Gloves with me in high school and became the IBF junior flyweight champion of the world in 1998. I'd sparred with him from the winter of 1994 through September 1996, until he won the USBA flyweight title and got world ranked in the top ten as a junior flyweight. That brings me back to the story of all the writing that got stolen from my car after I'd returned from my Seattle and Alaska fishing boat job, but I'm not quite ready to tell you the entirety of it yet. No, I'm remembering July 15, 2004, when I started the overnight shift at the shelter and the departing evening staff member left the TV on in the living room.

The shelter had just gotten a cable subscription, and the ESPN Friday Night Fights were on. I sat for a minute to see who was fighting, and the main event was being announced. Mohammed *The African Assassin* Kayongo, from Saint Paul, Minnesota by way of Kampala, Uganda, was fighting a ten-round match against José Antonio Ojeda at junior welterweight, my weight. In his corner was Tommy Brunette (God rest his soul) of the Brunette Boxing Gym in Saint Paul. Kayongo fought hard and well, as did Ojeda, going the distance for a ten-round draw. Wow, I thought, that's my goal. I want to get back in shape to the point that I spar with a guy on that level, who I see fighting ten-round fights on TV. Keeping that shelter job was only supposed to be my base, my springboard, while literary pugilism—getting writing work and training boxers—was supposed to be my staple. I fancied myself writing a best seller, moving to New York to hang out regularly with my aforementioned friend, Nick Bryant, who made his full-time living as a freelance writer and regularly dated aspiring supermodels he met in his neighborhood, West Greenwich Village, where he lived across the street from the famed jazz club, the Village Vanguard. I continued with the training business and ran regularly, working out almost daily. The following year, Grigsby, who'd lost his title in 1999 and a couple of years later served a prison sentence, was back in the gym, finishing out a three-fight contract with legendary promoter Don *Only in America* King. Grigsby won two fights and got a fight against the reigning IBF champion, José Victor Burgos. When I talked to him about it, he asked me to get our mutual trainer, Dennis

Presley, back for him. Presley returned to train Will, who regained the IBF junior flyweight title in May 2005. Also, my old teammate, Raúl Gracia, who was twenty-seven years old at the time, called and asked if I could get Dennis Presley to train him. He was deciding to turn professional. Dennis agreed, and I helped him, and when we took Raúl to spar with José Leo Moreno (who was thirty), a few weeks before Leo was going to fight Mohammed Kayongo for the Minnesota junior welterweight title in Saint Paul in June, I decided to rotate with Raúl in the sparring.

The first round went fine. Leo, a tough, solid Mexican American, who was being trained by my original coach, Emmett Yanez, who'd also trained Raúl at one point, was taking every punch I threw and coming steadily forward. I was dancing around and obviously controlling the ring. I remembered the first time I boxed him, around 1990 in an exhibition bout for the Saint Paul Winter Carnival, when I held back because we weren't competing for a decision, and I'd almost dropped him with my first solid punch. I felt good, thinking I'd done a great job the first round, deceptively convincing myself I could—at my current level of physical fitness—keep up the speed of movement and switch out after two rounds. Then, midway through the second round, I decided to take a break on the ropes and catch my breath. That's when Leo landed a solid shot—a right hand to the body—beneath my left pec, in the rib cage, the heart punch. This punch was my own specialty, which I still love, a powerful trademark turned back on me, one taught by the great Emmett Yanez (God rest his soul). I thought Leo had just broken my rib.

I made it through that round and said, "Okay, I'll let Raúl come back in." I pretended nothing happened and did pushups and sit-ups so no one knew I was hurt. I went into Urgent Care the next day and got X-Rays. My rib wasn't broken, the doctor said. Rather, Leo had torn my abdominal muscle. The doctor prescribed Percocet. I hate how Percocet makes me feel, and it hardly worked, anyway. I often worked out earlier in the day in between gym clients, and when we were training Raúl, I expressed frustration that I couldn't do sit-ups and stomach exercises because of this injury, so Dennis finally suggested an exercise for the upper abdominals—lying down, two-legged, bent knee raises—that wouldn't irritate that particular muscle. I questioned my prowess as a boxer, wondering if I could ever get back to sparring with guys on that level again. Meanwhile, José Leo Moreno dropped Mohammed Kayongo with body shots at the Saint Paul Armory on June 17, 2005, in the fourth round, winning the Minnesota junior welterweight title.

Leo was good. His final record was 12-2 (10 KOs). In February 2006, he fought a hard, competitive fight, losing a ten-round unanimous decision to Lamont Peterson for the World Boxing Council United States junior welterweight championship. Three years later, Peterson was champion of the world. Even though Peterson was a better boxer than Mohammed Kayongo, when I interviewed Leo for the

Upper Midwest Golden Gloves Yearbook, he told me Kayongo was "more of a manly fighter," because he slugged it out with him. That's the kind of fighter José Leo Moreno was.

Kayongo eventually ended up at the gym Grigsby opened and sparred a lot with Raúl. As a personal trainer at Uppercut Gym in Minneapolis, years later, in 2011, I did end up sparring with Kayongo a few times, going eight or nine rounds a session, as he prepared to travel for a ten-round fight in Uganda. At forty-two years old, when Kayongo was thirty-one, I told a priest in the confessional I was guilty of jeopardizing my health over pride. On the one hand, I boxed circles around him. On the other hand, he hit harder than anyone I ever sparred with, and the shots he did land took their toll. The last time I sparred with him, Dennis came by the gym to corner me, and Mohammed was visibly frustrated by his inability to handle my footwork. Dennis gave me great instructions and advice between rounds. Standing in the corner, listening to Dennis tell me—in a forceful yet almost whispering voice so only I could hear him—I was doing just fine, to "keep that jab in his face and keep moving," gave me all the confidence in the world. "He can't touch you, and he knows it. Man, it's driving him crazy!"

After the fourth round, Dennis built me up further, congratulating me on my superior ring generalship while encouraging my execution of punch combinations.

"Great, great—" he said as I returned to the corner standing and facing him and not even breathing hard as he gave me a shot of water over the ropes. "You got him right where you want him," he continued. "He can't figure you out. You're making him walk into shots, and you're in complete control; he can't catch you. Now this time, when you make him miss and fall off balance while you shuffle out from the ropes, take and put your right hand on his shoulder and give him a good push, just to let him know you can." Muffled laughter came from him with the last statement. He'd told me the right move to continue dominating, struggling through laughter as he did. I laughed, too, as the bell rang for the next round, then I did it.

His punches, however, were the kind that give world-class contenders problems. Roughly three weeks after my last sparring session with *The African Assassin*, it hurt too much to turn my head fully to the right, and a body blow to my left side was so damaging that I couldn't throw a right hand, because when it landed on the heavy bag, my *latissimus dorsi* muscle throbbed in stabbing pain. So, what does this story have to do with my need to finish and publish a book dedicated to Dad, using the talents God gave me and Dad helped me develop? Also, what other poems will it lead me into sharing with you? Well, it brings me back to August of 2007 when I first got involved at the National level with the National Writers Union.

I'd been elected a delegate by the Twin Cities Chapter of the Union. We called ourselves Chapters for some reason, probably because it works metaphorically as an expression of the type of amalgamated union we were, a bunch of freelance writers in Units (the term used by the UAW, which stands for United Auto Workers.) Our headquarters is in New York. I figured involvement at the national level would build connections on the East Coast, which is important if you want to move to New York. The National Delegates Assembly that year was in Boston, Massachusetts, at Emerson College.

I sat in Boston Commons Park, right across the street from Emerson College, the day before the conference began, reading the reports of the union officers while catching some sun. Also, I was, of course, enjoying the frequent appearance of pretty, young ladies walking through the park. On a rare weekend, not working that third shift shelter job, in the middle of a great American city full of beautiful women, I was enthused to say the least. I knew the likelihood of meeting by chance the girl of my dreams while on this trip was slim, but then again it was just as possible as it was impossible. Ambitious as I am and idealistic about having more than two children, I imagined meeting a younger woman who desired a large family and had years of fertility ahead of her. I literally said a prayer that I'd meet a woman around twenty-two years old. Less than five minutes later, I looked to my left and saw a young, petite lady with a jet-black ponytail and a smooth brown complexion pass by me from the left, my mouth immediately opening as I articulated a muffled "Hi," as she turned her head rightward, making split-second eye contact with me and quickly hurrying along.

Oh, I thought, I guess she's not interested. I watched her walk on about thirty yards before she circled around in a clockwise direction, ending up over my right shoulder about thirty yards away in the shade of a tree.

"Okay," I said to myself, "that's not what you're here for. You have to finish reading this External Organizing Vice President's report. If she's still sitting there afterwards, then you can talk to her."

She ate a sandwich she'd just bought as I read. I looked over a few times, and we smiled at each other. At one point, she even stood up and walked around in circles until, finally finished with my reading, I approached to greet her. We talked a good hour and a half and exchanged mobile phone numbers. She was a twenty-two-year-old, English-language college student from a mountainous village in Colombia, taking a year off from school to work as an au pair in Westchester County, New York. She was on a weeklong bus tour of historical sites on the East Coast. I took her to dinner that night. We found a place called Penang Malaysian Cuisine. I believe it was in the Hayden building on Washington at LaGrange Street. We shared a single dish of some type of squid along with fried rice if I remember correctly. We really enjoyed each other's company. She was short, petite, had this incredible smile and gorgeous, dark, hypnotic brown eyes. I gazed into them and thought, "Wow, what if nineteen or twenty years from now, we're finishing a meal like this together at this very restaurant, right after dropping off our firstborn son for his freshman year at Boston College?" Four months into my renewed commitment to my Catholic faith, following the rules, here I was, in love.

Dad happened to be in Westchester County at the time for the Military Order of the Purple Heart convention, and when my conference would end that Sunday, he was going to drive up and meet me. We stayed till the following Wednesday at Hanscom Air Force Base in Lexington, Massachusetts. He snapped a photo of me posing in a boxing stance in front of the Crispus Attucks statue in Boston Commons Park, and we went to the South Boston Boxing club, which I'd planned to do before I knew he'd be there to meet me. (I hadn't told him, but I'd been training for a planned professional fight that ended up falling through a month later.) We also visited his cousin, Maria, a professor at Brandeis University. When we checked out of the motel on the Air Force base, Dad left me at the bus station where, at his suggestion, I stored my bag in a locker and waited to meet my new Colombian love interest, who took the bus back to Boston to have lunch with me once more before I caught a cab to the airport and flew home.

I met with her for a couple of dates that December in Mamaroneck, the town where she lived and worked, during my annual stay with Nick in his Greenwich Village apartment. I took the train up, and she snuck away with the SUV of the couple she worked for, saying she was going to a company au pair meeting, two nights in a row. It was actually an innocent romance. We kept in touch, even though she was multiple states away. She was supposed to come visit me the following summer in July 2008, but that fell through. Luckily so, I guess. I mean, after all, I was recommitted to my Catholic faith, and she was going to stay with me, which would have been very tempting. Still, we kept in touch, first via email and then—after I accepted her invitation to join—Facebook. I was never going to get sucked into that information mining, digital mind trap, but between a combination of NWU leadership insisting that writers needed to utilize social media and the alure of the lady, I gave in. There were a couple of times when I was planning to visit Colombia and meet her family, but I saw some red flags. She was fallen away from the Faith, hooked up with some form of Pentecostalism. It's one thing if a girl grew up in a separated Christian community, but for someone who is already Catholic to have fallen away, it made her hostile to anyone who kept the Faith. So, no matter how drawn to each other we were, I couldn't and wouldn't cross that bridge. After all, the only reason the Connor line from which I descend is American is because my great grandfather's great grandfather—that's right, it traces that far back—was indentured to America under the Penal Laws, which lasted almost two hundred years in Ireland. We were American because the English made it illegal in Ireland to be Catholic. I couldn't commit to a woman who didn't respect that.

Needless to say, I met other women over the next ten years, leading to the events in my life that led to the poetry I've shared from between 2017 and 2019. Then, of course, while still trying to write and still trying to get things together as a Boxing trainer and finally follow through on my plan to move to New York and tap into its lucrative market, there was the sudden death of Dad. That is the most significant loss of my life. Sharing with you my observations of that time will lead me right into sharing with you the poem I've been delaying, the one about my writing from Seattle and Alaska being stolen. However, before I finally tell you that, I have to make an observation about the events that happened in the spring and summer of 2020, when I was still freshly mourning Dad and trying to reignite my literary pugilism pursuits.

First, the shutdown happened over the Corona Virus in March. The Chinese Communist Party is obviously responsible for that, and anyone denying it is either fooling oneself or lying. Then, of course, the incompetent Minneapolis city leadership collapsed in front of the world as rioting erupted. The day after the third precinct headquarters of the Minneapolis Police Department was burned down, I had stopped by the house to visit Mom. As I was talking to her, my phone vibrated with a message sent to me by Darwin Strong. He was asking if I could go to the Pow Wow Grounds Café and join up with the volunteers who were protecting the Native American Indian buildings in the neighborhood. I immediately typed back the answer, "Yes."

Mom asked about the message, and when I said Darwin asked me to help protect American Indian buildings, she said, "Please don't."

"I already told him 'Yes'," I said.

"Please don't bring your gun," she said.

I won't say any more about that conversation. Mike Goze of the American Indian Community Development Corporation, along with Bob Rice, owner of the Pow Wow Grounds Café, and Frank Paro, the new president of AIM, were coordinating the neighborhood patrol. People throughout the city of Minneapolis organized, many of them armed with guns and many of them not, to protect buildings and houses over the coming week. Gabby Strong sent me a message while I was on Franklin Avenue with the people protecting the neighborhood, telling me she was happy I was there. "Welcome to the revolution," she said. That could mean more than one thing. I know for a fact she didn't believe the rioters were righteous revolutionaries. I certainly don't either. I sent a message back to her. "I don't know about revolution," I said. "We have to be careful of vacuums." I wanted to write a poem about how I was protecting the neighborhood where my maternal grandparents were raised and married and my mom was born and baptized, at Holy Rosary, across the street from the Little Earth Housing projects, where an AIM barricade was set up and protected under armed guard. I wanted to write a poem about how I swung by the Aín Dah Yung transitional apartments on University Avenue, the street five blocks from where Dad grew up in St. Columba Parish. I wanted to explain in the poem how I stood with the people, but I wasn't with this protest that turned into so much destruction, and the only revolution I really support is the continuation of the Revolution of 1776, which established our country. I couldn't write any poetry about that week, though. I still haven't been able to. But I found a good one from 2004, one I performed to a cheering crowd on stage in front of the house band during an open mic hosted by nationally known Minneapolis spoken word artist Desdemona, at the Blue Nile Ethiopian restaurant, which had been Montanida's before, the restaurant where my maternal grandma had a party in 1945 when she'd decided to give up on men and join the convent and where, at the end of the party, sitting alone while the staff were cleaning up, a childhood friend (my grandpa), who'd served as a waist gunner on a B-17 bomber over Germany, showed up. He walked in with a flask of whiskey just wanting to talk, she said, and that was it for the convent. It's a Chinese restaurant now, not the Blue Nile, but I still remember sharing this poem there in February 2004, a bunch of the brothers with dreadlocks shouting their approval with my delivery.

I Feel the Eyes Upon Me
February, 2004, JMJ

I feel the eyes upon me,
and I know you are watching me—

I feel the eyes upon me,
and I know you are judging me!

I feel the eyes upon me,
but I am not here to harm you.

I feel the eyes upon me,
but I will not even disarm you.

I feel the eyes upon me,
but I am on a warrior path, and a warrior never kills over his own wrath.
I am on a warrior path, and a warrior never kills for sport.
I am on a warrior path, and a warrior always talks and finds a conflict
resolution.
I am on a warrior path, and a warrior knows there is almost always another
solution.
I am on a warrior path, and a warrior only kills as a last
resort.

I am Mark Connor,
initials, M.C.,
and, as I understand,
with a microphone in my hand,
I may even be referred to as an actual M.C.,
which would make me M.C., M.C.
Or better yet, MC squared,
which equals E—for energy—
which is the theory of relativity.
And everything's relative, man.

I don't know anytime what can you do?
What did he mean by, 'He sang his did; he danced his didn't'?
Who you trying to impress?
Remember, always do what you want to do, not what others want you to.
Remember what that old man told you, 'It's better to remain silent and be thought
a fool than to open your mouth and remove all doubt.'
Remember, you have been called Houdini in Reverse—you

can always get in—
you just can't get out.
Quit trying to figure everything out.
Maybe it's time to figure it all in.
Inside of you, that is.
It is so perverse—this structure of domination built on genocide and slavery—it is almost impossible to reverse without disintegration of all that is good along with all that is evil.
I just want to stand with and for the people, but I find myself isolated once again, through no fault of my own,
except for that I may just love too much.

I love you—too much!

I love all of you too much.

My brain, trying to keep me insane with instructions of how to use manipulation in order to gain
your cooperation
when I have learned from other circles that you must walk your own path, alone, the same as I must walk mine.
This doesn't mean that we aren't actually together or anyone must be left behind; it just means we must keep a healthy distance,
subordinating our individual vanities
in order to respect each other's individual humanity.

Do you remember that last fist fight you had with your brother,
the two of you bouncing punches off of each other,
him on the bottom and you on top,
crying with every blow you landed,
Ugghh—I love you—ugghh—Can't we—ugghh—please—ugghh—just—ugghh—stop?

You were both adults then, full grown men.

That was about him being one year older than you and still needing,
in his mind, to dominate you,
mentally torturing you because he could no longer do so physically, even though he still is pretty
physically
strong.

Son, it is not wrong for you to admit that,
in your relationships,
the reason you act in such a destructive way
is because throughout your life you have been abused—
mentally, physically, spiritually, and emotionally.
You might as well admit it, son, because it's the only way you're going to stop
yourself from constantly being used,
or at least from constantly being misunderstood.
Go on, admit it, son,
because it's the only way you're ever going to convince yourself that you actually
are good.
And son, there is no harm in admitting
that the man, six feet away
sitting
on that chair, his feet upon the footrest with the newspaper in front of him
ignoring the two of you is your father,
and you still love him,
and he loves you, too.

It is so perverse—this structure of domination built on genocide and slavery—
it is impossible to reverse
without disintegration of all that is good along with all that is evil.
I'm just going to stand with and for the people,
and not be isolated through any fault of my own,
except for that I may just love too much.
I love you, too much!
I love all of you—too much.

You feel the eyes upon you,
and you know I am watching you!

You feel the eyes upon you,
and you know I am judging you!

You feel the eyes upon you,
but you are not here to harm me.

You feel the eyes upon you,
but you will not even disarm me.

Conceptually speaking, *I Feel the Eyes Upon Me* came from something Kevin O'Rourke told me. This great, award winning, Irish American, Mississippi River barge-hand poet, who first took me to the Sundance community in 1995, taught me a lot over the years. He once said, "I walked into a place and thought everyone in the room was judging me, then I realized, by believing that, I was judging them." That's the whole point of the poem. In 2004, I had a misunderstanding with someone that was blowing up into a misunderstanding involving others, leading me to perceive myself being prejudicially objectified by people who misunderstood me. However, I was also misunderstanding them, which was also prejudicially objectifying them. Understanding this, I can walk among others with more confidence, reserving judgment, which delays condemnation, allowing everyone to function with more tranquility. But there is still a logical flaw in the poem.

The logical flaw is in my backwards recitation of the equation, $e=mc^2$. First of all, when I say, "M.C. M.C. equals mc^2," it does not. It actually would be $(mc)(mc)$, which is a different multiplication altogether, because the theory of relativity only multiplies M (which is Matter) by C (the Constant, the speed of light) after the Constant is squared (multiplied by itself). The crowd was fooled, though, believing I'd said something profound. They also thought it was profound and indisputable when I said everything is relative. Everything is not. Some things might be relative, for sure, but Truth isn't. Truth is the Truth even if no one believes it, and a lie is a lie even if everyone believes it.

That first week of summer 2020, every night as the curfew was placed on the Twin Cities, I was guarding neighborhoods with my friends, always within five blocks of where Mom is from in Minneapolis and part of the time in Saint Paul, roughly within five blocks of where Dad is from. I felt really good about that. It was the most purposeful thing I'd done in a long time. There was still, at least a brief moment every day, though, when I was alone in thought of Dad, taking my time to cry.

Yes, even, in the midst of protecting neighborhoods, exercising the Second Amendment guarantee of our God-given right to keep and bear arms and to organize ourselves in a well-regulated militia, I was mourning. When I had seen Dad lying in bed on life support, as I rubbed my rosary on his chest and forehead, I was more sorrowful for his experience of witnessing my succession of disappointments than for my own pain from seeing him die. How terrible it must be to watch your son come continuously close to making really big dreams come true, suddenly seeing them become sand slipping through his fingers and blowing into the whipping winds of time.

After one hundred and two amateur boxing matches, I left Saint Paul in the spring of 1994 and drove to suburban Seattle, Washington, staying with a friend of a friend. Every morning for three and a half weeks, I drove into Seattle and walked boat to boat looking for a fishing boat job. I was trying to get on a Salmon Seiner, the type of boat I was advised to seek work on by an experienced skipper from Minnesota, who owned his own gill net boat in Alaska. I eventually did gain employment on a Salmon Seiner that took me to Alaska for the summer. I wrote many stories and poems while in Seattle before and after the fishing season and many while in Alaska. I also wrote 170 pages of a first novel. After I got paid, I drove down the coast, visiting fishermen from other boats, friends from college, and someone who'd worked at the Alaska cannery where we'd sold our salmon during the season.

One of my California visits was to San Francisco. While there, I stopped into City Lights Books, the bookstore owned and operated by the Beat poet, Lawrence Ferlinghetti, author of *A Coney Island of the Mind*, a famous collection of poems. He also is fictionally represented as a character in novels by the King of the Beats, Jack Kerouac, author of *On the Road* and many other novels. Besides buying *Solitudes Crowded with Loneliness* and *The Ancient Rain* by Bob Kaufman, the lesser-known black Beat poet, I was looking for *Love in the Days of Rage*, a novel by Ferlinghetti. As I was standing in the Beat section at the top of the stairs on the second floor, I heard a man whose voice sounded familiar speaking to someone on staff as he walked up the stairs behind me. I turned around to see an old man with white hair and a beard, and I thought, that might be Lawrence Ferlinghetti. I turned back to the book rack and kept looking through the Lawrence Ferlinghetti books.

"Well, you're in the right section," I heard him say in a jovially encouraging voice.

"I know; that's why I came here," I said, sharing a smile with him. He entered the office and closed the door, so I turned back to the book rack.

I couldn't find the novel, so I knocked on the door.

The man opened up and looked at me.

"Yeees," he casually said with a semi-comedic smile.

"Excuse me, sir—" I said, "but what is your name?"

"I'm Ferlinghetti!" He smiled.

"That's what I thought," I said.

I told him I was looking for *Love in the Days of Rage*.

"That's out of print," he said.

"Oh," I heavily sighed, looking down in dejection.

He let a moment pass as I tried to look childishly disappointed.

"Let me see if I have any copies," he said reassuringly, closing the door.

He returned with a copy, holding it open, pointing to his autograph, saying, "This is one of my personal copies; I signed the inside."

"Thank you!" I smiled, standing there wanting him to tell me it was for free. "Wow," I said, "I really appreciate that." Then I just stood there looking at him.

"Ah, you can pay for that downstairs," he said, gently pointing.

"Okay." I smiled as he closed the door.

I had other stops to make after San Francisco—to my poet friend, Tony (the one who in *Irish Americans for Life* calls my girl "a lightweight goddess with auburn hair" and who, along with his wife, was getting a Masters in English at Claremont College, near L.A.), and to my great aunt May in Pasadena (whose daughter is the cousin, Maria, that Dad and I would visit in Boston in 2007). From there, I made a swing through L.A., a visit with my aunt in Las Vegas, a drive through Northern Arizona where I visited the cook from my skipper's brother's boat, then through New Mexico to Denver to meet a friend I'd known from Regis University, and finally a stop into the Rudé Center Boxing Club before heading home. I was back in Saint Paul in November, and although I was just supposed to be working on writing, I couldn't stay away from boxing, so by December, I was working out and regularly sparring with Will Grigsby. I'd normally stop at a coffee house after the gym and spend at least an hour or two, sometimes three or four, writing fiction before going home. I was writing my first novel. On Tuesday, February 28, 1995, I parked my four-door, light green, 1979 Pontiac Catalina on the southeast corner of Forest Street and Beech Street on the East Side, in front of Glancey's Gym. I was running a little late, and as I locked the doors, I looked at the passenger seat of the car where my maroon backpack was sitting. I should throw that in the trunk, I thought. No, it'll be okay. I ran into the gym and got ready so I could warm up, shadowbox, then spar with Will. I sparred 8 rounds with him that night. I did great, too. Will was getting ready for a fight at Mystic Lake Casino, the Medwakaton Dakota casino in Prior Lake, Minnesota, one of the far west suburbs. It was going to be broadcast on the USA Network's Tuesday Night Fights. My weight was back down to 139 pounds, my last fighting weight, and I figured, if I got down to 135 pounds, I could have some lightweight division professional fights in the coming months. Dennis Presley was impressed with my sparring as much as he was with Will's that night, and Will was really sharpening up and readying himself to progress towards world class competition. Dennis didn't want me to do it, and he even later told me he'd rather see me be a trainer and a writer, but he could tell I was planning to have some professional fights. Will and Dennis had already left, and I was using the shower as Jim Glancey got everything put away and was ready to head upstairs to his apartment for the night. I'd gotten dressed and was bundled up to go outside, where the temperature was below zero. I said goodbye to Glancey. I walked out to the sidewalk and noticed something shiny by the front of the car. As I got closer, I realized the shine I saw was the streetlight reflection of the broken glass from my passenger window, and in place of my maroon backpack was a red brick on the passenger seat. The personally signed Lawrence Ferlinghetti novel, *Love in the Days of Rage*, all my short stories and poems and journal entries in multiple notebooks, Bob Kaufman's *Solitudes Crowded with Loneliness*, a book given to me by a fisherman called *The Prophet* by Kalil Gibran, some other irreplaceable items, and of course the 170-page notebook manuscript of my first novel, were all gone.

I desperately looked in the alley, in dumpsters, but couldn't find it. Mom convinced me to go back one more time, the next day, letting her drive me; I looked through the alley again, and in a short time we gave up. The contents of the bag were most likely thrown away, but who knows where?

On March 7, 1995, Will Grigsby fought on the USA Network's Tuesday Night Fights at Mystic Lake. So did Quenton Osgood, making his light heavyweight debut. I was sparring partner to both of these guys and was with Dennis Presley in their corners. It was pretty cool, being on national TV like that, even if it was only cable. I met and shook hands that night with Thomas *Hit Man* Hearns. I also met the color commentator, former WBA lightweight champion *Irish* Seán O'Grady, one of my favorite fighters from the 1980s. Quenton won his fight by a knockout over a guy named Stacy Jameson. Grigsby got a little careless while he was pounding on Miguel Montoya from Mexico, a southpaw, as he measured him against the ropes and tried to land a big left hook, catching a straight left hand to the jaw that sent him face-first to the canvas. He got up, though, hanging on and fighting back to the bell. In the next round, he dropped Montoya and won by a TKO. I was excited to have been in the corner on TV. Dad asked me what I got paid. Nothing. When these guys made four hundred dollars for a fight and the trainer had a right to ten percent (and Dennis didn't take his cut that night), I didn't feel like asking for anything because I wasn't training them. I helped out here and there and sparred with them, but I wasn't officially fighting at the time, and if I did decide to have some fights, I'd get paid for that. But Dad was right. He was angry at me for sparring with guys without getting paid. Why should I put myself through the physical demands of sparring with guys if they didn't compensate me? I should have thought about that over the next week, but instead I was thinking about employment and about my lost writing.

I had briefly worked in the mail room of the Federal Department of Agriculture in downtown Saint Paul. It was okay, but the whole time there, I thought about writing and boxing, so I can't tell you much about it except that I sent mailings out to offices in counties across Minnesota. One old guy there was fascinated by the fact that I had worked on a fishing boat, and he kept telling me to go back. He seemed visibly trapped in his chair behind his desk in that office, an aging man with just a trace of his youth left, dreaming of adventure, dreaming of the freedom of possibility, looking out from behind his desk at the nothingness of the wall, seeing the clear waters off the deck of the fishing boat on which I'd worked, a child dreaming of one day living his grown-up desire of adventurous glory, finally breathing a sigh of fearful, docile acceptance that he was going to stay right there, in that chair behind that desk, responsible, safe, yet somehow disappointed over chances he did not take. I had just been laid off from that job, so I filed for unemployment, then I went to a coffeehouse to write.

I sat to write in the Hard Times Café, a collectively run coffeehouse at 1821 Riverside Avenue in Minneapolis. At the time, it was still a twenty-four-hour a day business (now they close from 4:00 a.m. to 6:00 a.m. and are open 22 hours a day, 7 days a week). I bought a cappuccino, poured some sugar into it, and sat just inside its main dining room on a stool at a counter at the western edge of the room, facing the espresso machine and coffee bar, with the front door to the right of my view, the tables behind me. The clientele of this place is decidedly avant-garde, a combination of punks, hippies, East African immigrants, Native American Indians, university students, transients and whatever else you can think of, converging on the edge of nowhere as if it were the center of the universe. I drank that cappuccino, and I wrote this poem.

America's Eyes, Ralph
March, 1995 JMJ

Sitting in the unemployment office on University Avenue,
    America,
I see the eyes of you –
the reddened whites centered
        with bright blues,
            all accentuated with dark bags of fatigue beneath them.
Everyone here seems so worried
        that they'll never find a job,
            never find that dull little spirit killer that gives them an identity.

But is that the thing by which I
    should be identified,
        Ralph Ellison?
I do not believe that you would agree
        with such a definition of reality,
            given your literary situation.
After all, you were the one
        putting paper to pen,
lending a voice to invisible men
        of all colors, shapes,
and sizes,
    you were the one who knew the desire to bump back
more often than not,
           aching with the need to prove to yourself
that you really did exist in the world.

    And tell me, Ralph – was Jack Kerouac
on to something when in the dingy neighborhoods
of Denver he wondered if death was anonymity
among men after all?
    And what does it matter, in the larger scheme of things,
if I live or die or stand or fall?
Does anyone have to read the novel that from my car
was stolen
    on February 28th, 1995,
            a brick going through my window
    on the East Side of Saint Paul while I was inside

a boxing gym helping my man, Will Grigsby,
     prepare to knock out Miguel Montoya on national
T.V. on March 7th,
          that thief running off with what's worth
so much more than money to me
  and nothing on the street?
If no one reads it, will I still exist?

It's not who I am, my coach would say –
It's what I do.
      Says the same thing about boxing too,
which is probably why he did so much better
  than I did,
    because he was only serious one year out of 25.

But still I'm here wondering if anyone cares
    that I'm alive,
        and whether I should care if they do.
Do I really want to be a legend, Ralph, like you—
or do I
    just want to tell the truth?

I just want to live forever,
    and the only way to do that, as far as I can see,
is to have a whole bunch of kids.
They could carry on a name for me,
    live on in gestures and body positions,
dream foolish dreams and make bad decisions.
Become writers or fighters or run away to sea.
      Or maybe they can lead peasant rebellions!
Anyway, I keep chasing my dreams.
I was writing a novel but someone stole it from
my car,
    and I was trying to become a world champion boxer
        when my Achilles tendons gave out.
    I'm doing both again, though,
              in spite of my doubts.
    $300.00 a week unemployment plus
    a cash job no one knows about,
leaving Jobs and Training and putting the reddened whites
of America's eyes, big blue and bright,
        outta my mind and outta my sight.

And I bow down to you, Ralph Ellison,
    in the coffee dream of the night,
respecting your longevity which I know will beat that
       of the great American Beat bard,
      strolling around the railroad yard,
singing his drunken vision of the American night
     found at the bottom of the cloudy waters
        of a bottle of Thunderbird.

Before I'm dead,
          my man,
   my voice will be heard,
no matter what I do—
              I'm going to leave my mark,
                    just like you.

After writing that poem I wrote a letter to Lawrence Ferlinghetti and mailed it, along with the poem, to him. I recounted the story of how I'd met him and bought the Kaufman books and the autographed copy of *Love in the Days of Rage* from him. I told him how my notebook manuscript of my novel along with all the other unrecoverable writing was stolen with other books and irreplaceable material. "There's nothing you can do about the novel," I told him. "I'm not crying about it. I did that when it was stolen. It's my responsibility now to rewrite it." The one thing I did hope he would do, though, was send to me another copy of *Love in the Days of Rage* and Kaufman's *Solitudes Crowded with Loneliness*, for which, I explained, I was willing to pay. It must have been a month that went by. I was renting a room in a house in Saint Paul owned by an Irish American activist, who'd been alerted by the mailman that he'd been instructed by his supervisor to write down and report the return address to every piece of mail delivered there. So it was no surprise to me that I got a white envelope from City Lights Books with the upper corner torn open. Ferlinghetti is a politically professed Anarchist, and Irish Republicans from Ireland frequently stayed at the house, so I figured the mail had been tampered with. I opened the envelope and found two books. One was Kaufman's *Solitudes Crowded with Loneliness* and the other was the book with which Ferlinghetti launched his City Lights Books, *Pictures of the Gone World.* Inside *Pictures of the Gone World* was Lawrence Ferlinghetti's autograph preceded by the declaration: "For Mark Connor, who will make his mark."

Imagine that. I don't know if *America's Eyes, Ralph* is the greatest poem, and I've never convinced someone to pay to publish it, but the great poet, Lawrence Ferlinghetti, autographed his own book while quoting my poem back to me. That felt really good.

V

The day Dad died, Monday, September 30, 2019, after we left the hospital, Mom and I checked into the Marines' Memorial Club, where they'd been staying and had checked out ten days earlier, when ready to come home. She and David had checked back in there the previous Monday, September 23, after he'd flown to San Francisco to join her at the hospital, then checked out again when he returned home on Friday, September 27. They'd gotten a cramped room. But seeing how her husband had just died and we were going to be arranging to fly him home, they gave us a suite at single room price. Of course, we flew Dad home whole, for burial. He had already bought his and Mom's funerals ten years earlier, utilizing a veteran's discount through the DAV, and bought an insurance policy that would fly either one of them home from anywhere in the world. That is serious good fortune; it was all planned out, all prepared for long in advance, even though no one ever knows the day or the hour.

The first time I'd been to San Francisco was when I was nine years old in 1978, when Dad and Mom drove us there for the National DAV Convention. We stayed in the Holiday Inn, and the Convention was at the San Francisco Hilton Hotel inside the Centennial Ballroom. Mom explained that to me as we ate in the Marines' Memorial Club Leatherneck lounge on the top floor because, although I remember that trip well, I was too young to remember all the details. I guess Dad looked into membership at that time but couldn't afford it in his younger years. But when my cousin, Alexius, a lawyer living in the Hayes Valley neighborhood, canceled her wedding in May 2009 (thankfully she met a much better man and married in 2014), Dad suggested that, since the family event was canceled, he and I go visit her. We'd stay in the Marines' Memorial Club a couple of days, and then I'd hang out a few days more with her when he went home. I hung out with David McMillan, too, a high school classmate who became a structural engineer and settled in the city with his lady, Erika. That was the last year I worked the overnight job at the shelter, and it was the first vacation I'd had in a while. I spent a week in San Francisco and flew for a few days to Los Angeles, where I worked out in Freddie Roach's Wild Card Gym in Hollywood. A few years earlier, Dad had gotten a Benefactor membership in the club at a real cut-rate price before it doubled. As his son, I had the right to join at no added cost, so Dad insisted I get a membership, which I did. The Marines' Memorial Club is a great place. It was established for veterans of all branches to honor them and their families, especially families of those who died for our country. As I provided information to generate my card, the woman taking the information asked if I ever served in the military.

"No," I said. She noted that as she continued the process.

Later, I told Dad that it bothered me, realizing I was getting a benefit through his past service, even though I hadn't served. There had been a few times in my life when I was in both Army and Marine recruiter's offices, one time even holding a pen over the dotted line to sign a commitment to join the Marines at age sixteen, but I put the pen down and said I had to think about it then never went back. That, I said, made me feel guilty.

"Don't let that make you feel guilty," he said. "Just let it remind you to respect those who did serve even more."

That was my third time in San Francisco. Now I was here with Mom, my fourth time, to watch Dad die. I had to be responsible, with her, for getting him home. How easy it was, having parents like I do, because it was already arranged. Mom is imminently competent, too. I can't imagine how devastating it was for her to lose her husband, who had been married to her for exactly fifty-one years, seven months, and seven days. Nanette Jane Swanson became Mrs. Nanette Connor on February 23, 1968. She was the first person in her family ever to go to college, and she went from being a school teacher to working in communications and grant management in a few Saint Paul City departments, attending law school at night between my 7th and 10th grade years, becoming a lawyer, and working various state government positions, so when it came to handling paperwork and arranging the logistics to get Dad home, she had no problem. The other reality, though, that helped her so much in dealing with this situation, is her faith, not just her faith in God to be there and help her through this and to bring Dad safely home to Heaven, but her faith she shared with Dad, the faith that brought them together, the faith that revealed to them their vocation, to be married, to share God—who is in fact Love—with each other, the vocation, as I earlier recounted Dad telling me at breakfast, so necessary for two people to decide to marry responsibly.

David McMillan connected with me this time, too, buying me dinner the night before Dad died and hanging out with me in the Leatherneck Lounge afterwards, talking about his own father, another Marines' Memorial Club member, who died some years earlier.

The summer of 2019 was chaos for me, a chaos that had been building since 2017. Every time it seemed I was finally stabilizing my progress towards securing a regular living as a boxing trainer combined with income as a writer, my boat got rocked in a manner threatening to capsize all my plans, or so it seemed. As I said, though, early on, the Guardian Angels were watching out for my parents and were also watching out for me.

I had rented an office at Element Gym, storing my equipment there, keeping files on personal training clients, spending time there reading and writing and planning my future. When we had fight cards at Element, I would wrap boxers' hands in my office and give them pep talks before they went into competition. But the gym expanded in 2019, moving to a larger space on the other end of the building, nearly doubling its rent, which meant doubling the rent of sublets, which meant I could no longer afford it. I continued on without an office. In need of any extra money I could get, I took a temporary job with the Census Bureau, verifying addresses across Minnesota in preparation for the actual Census count in 2020.

In late July, having breakfast with Dad and spending time with him and Mom at the house afterwards, I told him I'd bought a ticket to see a play at St. Patrick's Catholic Church on Desoto Street on the East Side. The Franciscan Brothers of Peace are housed there, as well as at the old convent at St. Columba, Dad's boyhood parish. In 2018, I'd introduced myself to Brother Pascal, a skinny young guy in his early thirties, who was in line at the post office wearing his Franciscan robe. He lived at St. Columba, and I periodically talked to him and once even helped at their foodbank. The play at St. Patrick's was called *Thank God Ahead of Time* and was a biography of Blessed Solanus Casey, a Franciscan Friar from an Irish immigrant family in Prescott, Wisconsin, who ended up a "Simplex Priest" in Michigan and New York, meaning a priest allowed to say Mass but not to preach homilies and hear confessions. However, he could pray and was known to give good, simple, holy advice, and many miracles were attributed to his prayers. In fact, people wrote him from around the country and even the world, asking his prayers and reporting that, after asking his prayers, many cures and resolutions to terrible problems were received. Understanding the stress I'd been under, Dad was happy I was going to the play that night. In the chapel behind the auditorium, an opportunity was given to observe a relic of Blessed Solanus Casey. I touched my rosary to it. The relic was a piece of hair from Casey's long beard, preserved in a glass casing. Protestants freak out about stuff like this, and I fully understand why. There is a great danger of becoming superstitious with relics. My American Indian friends are more comfortable with this type of practice because it's similar to things they do—as I mentioned earlier—in the sweat lodge or the Sundance or any time praying, asking their departed relatives to pray for them and bring their prayers to God. When I found out on Saturday, September 28, that I had to rush to San Francisco, I stopped by St. Columba to talk to Brother Pascal and ask for prayers. I sat in the parking lot, facing the house Dad grew up in across the street, calling on my mobile phone to find a ticket for the soonest flight out. Dave Bonniwell, a retired Ramsey County Sheriff's deputy who grew up with Dad, had spoken to me a little earlier. His wife, Kathy, is a retired ticket agent at Delta Airlines. I hung up from an online discount ticket agent and was considering the flight when a call from Dave Bonniwell came through.

"Don't worry about a ticket, Mark," he said. "We'll book one for you right now, and we're paying for it."

They got me a flight for ten o'clock that night.

The Guardian Angels were looking out for us. The faith Mom and Dad grew up with was leading us.

"Don't worry about getting to the airport, Mark; I'll pick you up, and you'll have spaghetti for dinner with me and Kathy, then I'll drive you there."

The city of Saint Paul. My home. I'd been trying to leave it for years. As I said much earlier, in late October 2018, I was in New York when my friend, Dakota spiritual leader Art Owen, died. I was staying with my musician friend, Dan Barrett, running around Manhattan and Brooklyn and Queens for two weeks, visiting every Boxing gym I could to discuss the possibility of being a trainer out there. I visited with my friend, Ricky Ray Taylor, who'd been making a good living at it for the last seventeen years. Fifteen days before the heart attack, I talked to Dad in my departed Uncle Tom's house, which he was trying to clean up to get a better price on it for my cousins. He'd just recently gotten an ablation on his heart at the V.A. Hospital to try to regulate its beat, but it didn't work. Still, they okayed him to travel.

"It's almost a year since I was in New York, Dad," I said. "On that trip, for the first time, I really felt like I could move there and make a living, then one hassle after another has delayed me. Then you had to go in for the ablation last week, and it really scared me. I really thought you could die. What if I move to New York and you have a heart attack?"

"That's what planes are for," he said.

"Yeah, I guess you're right."

The truth is, he was always right.

"You have to live your life," he said. "If you want to go there, do it."

There I was, in the parking lot, basically the playground he grew up on, across the street from the family house in the parish where he was raised. Prayers were promised from the Franciscans, and I was going to see him and pray for him in the city named after St. Francis. That's what planes are for.

Dave Bonniwell picked me up and took me to his house, where his wife, Kathy, was waiting with Dad's other childhood friend, my Godfather, Tom Stephani and his wife, Pam, and we ate spaghetti together, then they drove me to the airport.

Yes, the Guardian Angels were watching out for Mom and Dad and for all of us. How can that be, you might ask, when Dad ended up dying anyway?

Remember, St. Joseph, most chaste Spouse of the Blessed Virgin Mary and earthly father of Jesus Christ, is the patron of a happy death. Tradition presumes he died with Jesus and Mary at his side. That's the best presumption to make. However, his whole life must have been so wonderful. Imagine, not only are you chosen to be the matrimonial companion to the greatest mortal human being in all eternity, but your son is God. When it finally comes time to pass from this world into eternity, how can you not be overjoyed at the wonderful life you've been privileged to live and ecstatic with the knowledge that you now will live in perpetually increasing love and joy for eternity? Dad died with his family around him. David got to be there for five solid days, played recordings of his grandchildren in his ear, and I was there with Mom praying over him. And he had that St. Christopher medal around his neck. Saint Joseph went through a lot of difficulty, not the least of which was the terror of having to protect Jesus and Mary, fleeing with them to Egypt when Herod was killing the holy innocents, all the boys two years old or younger, in an attempt to kill Jesus. Dad went through his difficulties, the most dangerous being the Vietnam War, but also many other challenges in life, including helping his brothers and sisters, doing a lot to take care of his parents and family. But he enjoyed life every moment, knew how to laugh, was always good to people, and he got his last rites and the Apostolic Pardon with his wife and son there. That's how the Guardian Angels were watching over Mom and Dad at the time of his heart attack and, ten days later, the moment of his death. But the Guardian Angels were watching over all of us always, as I can see in other events of years past.

Mom told me that she couldn't complain. She had a happy marriage and a very lucky life. She didn't feel instantly in love when they first met but somehow knew they would get married, she has told me many times. Also, one thing that really attracted her to him was that he had such kind friends. They made her feel so comfortable. She'd love to have him around for decades more, but she is grateful for all the years he was here. Not only that, but he always protected her, and you could even say he's the reason she's still here.

In the fall of 2014, Dad and Mom went on a trip following the path of Saint Paul's travels from Turkey to Greece. I drove them to the airport, the way I always did. After I'd put their luggage in my car and they put on their coats and we were ready to walk out the door, Mom took me to the kitchen and pointed towards the entrance to the dining room, saying, "Over there on the dining room table are the legal documents and papers explaining exactly what to do to bring home either of our bodies if one of us dies on this trip."

"Mom," I said, "stop saying that! You're coming home."

I was so upset with her when she said that to me. For that trip, she'd been telling me over and over again that preparations had been made in case something happened. Who expects something to happen?

So, there I was, between 1:30 and 2:00 p.m. on Sunday, October 26, 2014, in Nina's Café on Selby and Western Avenues, just up the street from the Cathedral of Saint Paul, where I'd attended Sunday Mass. I was reading a book of short stories, *Rope Burns* by F. X. Toole, given to me by Dennis McGrath, the public relations guru and former boxing writer I mentioned earlier. The story I was on is *Million Dollar Baby*, the one made into an Academy-award-winning movie. I was at the point in the story where the first-generation Irish American trainer visited his female boxer in the hospital, who'd been paralyzed by a cheating opponent who attacked her from behind, after the bell, when the round was over. This boxer asked her trainer to remove the machines keeping her alive, and he refused and left the hospital. That's when I looked at my mobile phone and saw a message from David.

"I guess Mom's in the hospital in Greece. It looks serious."

I closed the book, got my jacket on, rushed home, and started making calls. I informed Mom's sisters and did my best to contact Dad. I couldn't actually talk to him till that night, and he said they had her in the intensive care unit and wouldn't tell him anything. They'd been on a boat from Rhodes to Ephesus, and Mom was physically troubled enough that Dad called the boat's doctor, who immediately had the captain turn the boat around to return to Rhodes. At one point, the same close friend, Dave Bonniwell, talked to Dad and said he'd never heard him sound so scared. Anyway, after talking with Dad, I decided I'd have to try to do what I would normally do as I got ready for bed and keep praying. I'd been praying to St. Jude from the moment I heard Mom was in trouble, going back and forth between begging God to keep Mom alive and make everything okay and begging St. Jude to keep up that begging for me. My family, on both sides, always prayed to St. Jude.

I laid down in bed with a reading lamp on, returning to the *Million Dollar Baby* story. I opened up to where I left off. The trainer stepped out of a taxi in front of St. Brendan's Catholic church, where his first-generation Irish American childhood friend was a priest to whom he went for weekly confession. The narration said, "It was October 28, the Feast of St. Jude."

I took it as a sign. St. Jude was watching over Mom and Dad. Things would be okay. But I still kept praying, of course, to St. Jude to pray for us, along with constant Hail Marys, and just begging God. Over the next day, I tried to communicate with Dad when I could and found out Mom had suffered internal bleeding. She had a bleeding ulcer. They also found heart problems that would have to be taken care of later. On Tuesday morning, I got a text message from her saying she was okay, and Dad would get them home. That just happened to be October 28, the Feast Day of St. Jude.

Mom and Dad were supposed to be home on Halloween, but because of the medical emergency, they didn't get back until the following Friday, November 7. I told them the story of hearing about her as I drove them home. As I brought in their luggage and discussed with Mom how I'd been praying to St. Jude, then discovered that I found out about her just before reaching the St. Jude part of the story, followed by her recovery on the Feast Day of St. Jude, just as we got inside the door and closed it behind us, she said, "Let me show you this."

She dug through her purse. Eventually, she pulled out an old piece of paper, unfolded it, and handed it to me.

It was the prayer of St. Jude.

"Wow," I said.

"Your Grandma Connor gave that to me on our wedding day."

"Really?"

"Yeah."

"And you've carried it with you ever since?"

"Yes, I have," she said.

You might think it doesn't mean anything. I know one thing for sure, it gives me comfort. I believe in the Communion of Saints. Maybe some people don't, but there's someone I know who does, and that one is God.

I told you I'd been in New York, almost a year before Dad died, to explore places where I might be able to train boxers. Every time I visit the city, I visit the oldest and most prestigious gym there is, Gleason's Gym. I did that at least twice a year from 2009 through 2015 as a Trustee of the National Writers Union. I had to conduct semi-annual audits with one of the other two Trustees and always stayed a few extra days to visit friends and make it to Gleason's. After I'd left Gleason's in the winter of 2015, I stopped for a slice of pizza across the street and wrote the following poem when I saw a woman experiencing obvious trouble.

Ten Minutes
January, 2015 JMJ

This poor red-haired woman—
    wandering rapidly up Washington Street,
    turning onto the sidewalk of Front Street,
    left hand swinging frantically
    back and forth, wearing last night's white and
    black paisley stretch-pants and
    zipped up imitation letterman's jacket—
                searches desperately
                with desolate eyes
                behind petite glasses
                for some stranger's dollar.
I saw her pass by just now,
    pushing haplessly on
            somehow,
    not knowing that to just give up
            will help her finally win,
            let the loser finally begin
            to taste victory.
I think of Father
    last night,
    looking younger than I am,
    at St. Patrick's Cathedral,
    telling me before granting me absolution
    to step towards my life's solution
    with the prescribed penance
    of sitting for ten minutes and thinking
    of all for which I am grateful.
"That's all God asks," he says, "ten minutes."
            A good Father knows the limits
                of His children.
It's been ten days in New York,
        and I return to freezing cold Saint Paul
        tomorrow.
        But the weather here—
        while crisp and clear
        in the absence of snow—
        is still windy and cold.
I am grateful for Mom's survival
from a near death medical emergency
on a pilgrimage of Saint Paul's footsteps.

VI

I'm pretty close to making my point with this book, but before I reach my conclusion, I offer another story, one I almost forgot to include, giving me hope, that virtue I said I always cling to, in spite of my attitude that often seems sad and doomed to gloom. It's about Nancy, the daughter of my lawyer friend, Bob Dildine.

Remember my novel getting stolen and how I wrote the poem, *America's Eyes, Ralph*, at the Hard Times Café in Minneapolis? Well, in 2000, that café got shut down and spent a couple of years fighting to stay open because the president of their collective got arrested for providing twenty dollars-worth of marijuana to a young lady cop. Bob Dildine, a prominent local immigration lawyer, who rented an office upstairs from the café, represented them in court. Since this collectively run business generated very little money, he charged them what they made as an hourly rate, which was five dollars, plus a free meal whenever he wanted. I wrote a bunch of articles for the local alternative paper covering the story and got to know Bob. One time, I visited him in his home and his daughter, Nancy, was there.

Nancy was gorgeous. Her mom was a Haitian immigrant whom Bob represented in immigration court so she could stay in the country. I don't know all the details, but Bob ended up adopting Nancy, and I believe her mom died at an early age. Bob was over fifty when I met him, and Nancy was grown up. One day, I stopped by Bob's place to talk to him. Nancy was there, and we three talked for hours. I found her attractive, though I didn't think of her romantically. Time went by, and I lost track of her. But one day, around the transition to summer from spring 2006, I was at the Hard Times for Irish tea, and Nancy was in line with me. We shared a smile, and I was just happy to see her. Our brief conversation was slightly flirtatious. Later, I thought, the next time I see her, I'll ask her out. At least two, maybe three, weeks went by without seeing her, so I wondered about her.

I saw Ken, a Hawaiian guy who was friends with Bob and was among the regulars who played the Chinese board game called Go, as well as Chess, at the café. I asked him if he'd seen Nancy.

"Didn't you hear?" he asked.

"No," I said, "hear what?"

"She died two weeks ago."

She had kidney issues. She had her whole life in front of her. She had just graduated the University of Minnesota with majors in French and International Relations, and instead of working for the United Nations as she'd planned, she'd started executive training at Target Corporation because of her health. In for dialysis one day, she had complications and died. She was twenty-five. I was thirty-six and don't know if anything would have materialized between us. I just know she was a pretty special person, and God took her when He saw fit. I also know it devastated Bob, who was never married and had no other children. In his pain, he returned to a place he'd been in his younger years, Taiwan, where he'd taught English, I believe to college students and possibly corporate employees. In a fortunate turn of events, he reconnected with a lady there, Fionn. They married and had two sons, who at the writing of this book were turning fourteen and eleven. I sent Bob an email so I could include this story in the book. He answered me from Taiwan.

"I still feel the tragic loss," he told me. "Have no regrets, just a fond memory of a beautiful powerhouse of a woman … I think Ken has died as well. You, though, are still young. Younger than me when I started a second family."

Thank you, Bob, for the encouragement and for being an example of a man who moves on and lives gratefully, honoring the value of love, family, and life.

This is not a novel, but I may write fiction based on these experiences. I withhold certain details, disguising people's identities, like my Halfway Around girl, whose name and job and how we met aren't mentioned. Today, people distort reality by manipulating language for the purpose of destroying whatever they can for their perverse perception of power, making protection of the vulnerable just as—if not more—important than ever. Knowing a man found love and marriage and family in older age inspires me, countering the dictatorship of relativism with which we are constantly bombarded, protecting me from shame over my affection for others. I'm not defeated in the loss of possibilities with others, knowing my love for them increases with acceptance of God's will and the passionate wish for them to experience it.

That's the way it was with her in *Halfway Around*, as with so many others. I was rooting for her. I read all 515 pages of *Women Who Run with the Wolves* with the wish to discuss all of it with her, including all the notes, amounting to 582 pages, but it seems too overwhelming to reread that book now, so I can't explain to you, my reader, exactly what it's about. I didn't agree with everything the author said, and I know our intended discussion would have led to a mutual examination of relationship between people, in general, and woman and man, specifically, allowing for revelations internally and externally for each of us mutually, individually, independently, and together, open to epiphany, a conversation rooted in honesty and united with truth.

Like I said, I was rooting for her. Emotionally, I feel the eyes upon me, so I perceive a demand to explain my love for her to the world, as if I must apologize for something in my nature, given me by God. I owe no explanation to the "Super

Trad" Catholic whose insecure accusation lies in a heart as human as its dictatorial counter, claiming her youthful choice to be superior to the sacred impossibility twisted into the desecration of the fundamentalist.

She's not the first open lesbian woman to whom I've been attracted or with whom I've become platonically—and even romantically—close; under the right circumstances, she wouldn't be the only one with whom I've shared a romantic kiss, either. I don't blame her for walking away from me, though, because from the tyrannical view fostered within the Empire of Fear, a man respecting her is impossible, and to trust one who claims to would violate the arbitrary laws dictated by relativism. Little does she know that a man respecting and living out true manhood would discuss that book with her, delight in the sound of her voice and expressions on her face, and love her fraternally and romantically to whatever degree appropriate according to the mutually discerned will of God, encouraging her growth mentally, physically, spiritually, and emotionally, even in her love for women to the point that she may see the benefit of transforming her sterile erotic desires into a fruitful sisterhood fostering a garden in which their respective children, guided by their honorable, protective fathers who sacrifice their lives in love for them, may happily play, growing into the seventh generation of love, family, and life.

"Yeah, that's just a fantasy," you might say. "The woman you describe would never do that, and the man you describe is too weak."

"True," I'd say to you, "but it wouldn't be she who creates that reality or me to whom the responsibility of directing it is assigned. Rather, that strongest of women, that vessel of God, that monstrance of salvation gently, firmly, embracingly guiding us with her final words—'Do whatever He tells you,'—will form for us the plan, and we will follow the rules already provided us, respecting creation and honoring the Creator. Not reinventing the wheel; just being separate spokes united in the center so life can go on."

VII

In following this story and reading my poetry, depending on who you are, you've probably found some observations—hopefully many observations—with which you agree. You've probably also found some with which you disagree. You may find my love for Dad and my relationship with him good and admirable, you may be ambivalent to them, or you may even be repelled by them. The whole book, from the first to the last word, is about time. It's about the limitations of time and the gift of time and about gratefully and prudently using time. It's about honoring time and honoring people within time, and it's about doing what should have been done a long time ago, so you can call the book *It's About Time*. Some realities mentioned earlier in this book have not been fully revealed, and I want to explain some key points so I am not misunderstood, as a man, in order that people can make up their own minds about what I say.

Obviously, much of this poetry is written to women with whom I've been either romantically involved or to whom I've just been attracted. In 2019, I was invited to share poems at the annual St. Patrick's Day party a family has thrown at St. Mark's Parish for more than fifty years. It was the first time I'd ever been there, and I recited the first three, *The Perfect Metaphor, Ever Since,* and *Two Pilgrim Souls, Anam Cara*. An old man around Dad's age approached me afterwards, and we stepped outside and talked a little about the poems. He really liked them and encouraged me to keep writing. He also asked me about my faith and about my desire to find a woman to marry. He admired the poems for their quality and linguistic clarity, but he had one caution.

"They could be dangerous," he said.

"I know that," I told him. "They could be used for seduction. I don't do that."

It's true, I don't. The women I've mentioned, the women to whom I've written the romantic poems, are all younger than I am, and a couple of them are significantly younger. If a man desires to father children, there must be a limit to the age of women he courts, and as each year goes by, that age limit gets one more year younger than his own age, until, God forbid, it gets too late. It's just a reality of life. One of the sickest incongruencies of modern life is that people generally are more comfortable publicly sharing information about their sex lives than about their financial lives. They're either afraid people will think less of them for making too little money, or they'll try to exploit them or cause them trouble if they make too much money, but they feel fine letting people know they're sexually involved. They're ashamed to admit to striving for moral chastity, though. I told you at the beginning of the book that I'm Catholic, and I said that, in 2007, I fully returned to the faith, began praying the rosary daily and decided to avoid casual relationships. I started following the rules, all of them. You can make any presumption about a poem based on its text and should be able to imagine different people involved in situations described within them. So if the text of the poem portrays a greater or lesser degree of intimacy within its story, so long as you can critically prove it with quotes from the text, feel free to let your mind wander there. That's part of the achievement of universality in a well-written poem. Know with certainty, though, if you try to assign any autobiographical realities between me and the women about whom I wrote these poems, that it never happened with any of them. Especially since 2007, that has been my choice, because I am a Godfather to my niece and a Confirmation Sponsor to her and her brother, and that is the standard up to which I must live. If I fall, I must get back up. That's the standard required of any honest Catholic as it is the standard of any honest Sundancer.

It may seem strange to compare the honest Catholic to the honest Sundancer. Remember the line, though, in my poem *Halfway Around*, referring to "mutually multiple pleasures of a mental, physical, spiritual, and emotional nature, peaking at the point of merger of difference and unity." In 1993, I listened to a lecture at the Minnesota Zen Meditation Center by Shoaku Okumura, a Japanese Soto Zen monk, called *Living in Vow at the Point of Merger of Difference and Unity*. I wasn't becoming a Buddhist. I was just trying to calm my mind and learn better concentration for boxing. However, I've carried that concept with me. We have differences, but a point of truth brings us together, where we unite, while keeping our own identity. The mental, physical, spiritual, and emotional elements are the four portions that comprise each human being. The Medicine Wheel, which represents in color—red, white, yellow, and black—all the people of the world, also represents each of those four elements. The circle is always turning, and one element or another may be the central experience of the moment, but they are all there, all the time.

One point of merger of difference and unity is the respect for family and the value of sex. Those who believe sex is meant for arbitrary enjoyment in the absence of commitment, who believe in polyamory, approve of, produce, distribute pornography and/or broker prostitution, do not value sex. No, those who value sex are those who confine it to the commitment of husband and wife, who, making love, form family. If you think that's prudish, you're crazy. If God ever grants me a wife, I'm perfectly comfortable going through every page of the Kama Sutra and exploring Taoist Tantric techniques with her, so long as we're natural and open to life. Those who value sex never put a price on it because it cannot be bought or sold because, in fact, sex is not a commodity. Humans are not a commodity. We are priceless, and sex is a gift to be shared only in love that is never lustful because it is never selfish and is always selfless. Sex is sacred.

"People don't understand," Ray Owen said to me back when I went with him and Art and Darwin to the Sundance. "We're more conservative than the Republicans."

He wasn't talking about every political issue, but he was definitely talking about the sanctity of the human body. Art said the same thing, too. I believe it's probably because their late father—Amos, whom I never met—said the same thing to the hippies who flocked out to Prairie Island after he started the sobriety sweat there in the 1980s. He opened it up to people outside the Native American Indian community, and the hippies gravitated that way, bringing with them the libertine tendencies of the progressive ideology. It's similar to how progressives supported Irish freedom but wished to discard the Catholic—as well as protestant—values within the Irish Republican cause.

So, the comparison is made between honest Catholics and honest Sundancers. Oftentimes, I remember exact dates of events in my life and recall them to the listener when I tell the story of those memories. I can't recall exactly when I had this specific conversation with Dad, though. I asked if he was worried if I followed American Indian traditions and abandoned the practice of the Catholic faith.

"I can't do anything about that," he said. "You're an adult. You have to make that decision yourself."

It's funny how things work out. I always had this calling in my heart I could hear from God. I was always longing for Him. I always thought of God as being the presence that centered and stabilized my family but also everyone in my world, holding together the circle in my life wherein I have concentrated my personal love. Some of those people, in fact probably an unusually large number of those people, ended up in prison, dead, or both. Also, an unusually large number ended up in overwhelmingly fortunate situations. I can't say the following poem is directly related to the aforementioned conversation with Dad about the Catholic faith verses the Red Road, but I can say it's about time and about integrity and about using God's gifts. I also think it's one last thing to contemplate, something from way back in 2004, that helps me understand my conclusions reached when reluctantly letting Dad go, trusting him confidently to God.

A Man Keeping His Fantasies
August 12, 2004, JMJ

A man keeping his fantasies is one who gives up his dreams,
    trading them away for the con of the promise of someday.

    Of course, that someday never comes,
        or really if it ever arrives, it's just here right now,
        and you've fooled yourself into missing it.
    The one keeping the fantasy continues to wallow in it,
        pathetically insisting to others against his own doubts
        that his grand plans really are going to work out,
        knowing at least subconsciously in his frightened heart
        that time keeps moving right along,
          whether you are or not.

    You can work right now on your great dream,
        or you can put off that responsibility
        for destructive self-indulgence in hallucination
        of what one is too afraid to try to make happen,
        of demons who will come back to haunt you
        with the acceleration of old age into premature death.

    Some people are more desperate than others,
        so they do this at a much earlier age,
        bringing themselves to ruin through prison or death,
        because violence and alcohol and drugs are the only means
        by which they can seem
            to cope with their fear,
            and rarely is someone smart enough
        to delay gratification in the midst of these three
        distractions
          long enough
            to turn them into a viable future
                on which to build
                outwardly legitimate action.

In a conversation Dad and I had during one of our weekly breakfasts, I told him how I remembered being at Mass when I was as young as three, maybe four. I remember being on the ground, looking down at the kneeler in the pew a few rows back from the altar, in the northeast corner of the basement church at St. Pascal, by the Conway Street entrance. I was whining a bit, and Dad put his hands on my shoulders and calmed me, and I steadied myself and looked up at the priest, who was in the middle of his homily.

"God is always calling us to Him," he said, "reaching out to us, and we are always longing for him."

"You can remember that far back?" he asked.

"Yes," I said.

"That's a real grace, Mark," he said.

"Really?"

"Yeah. You have a real gift of faith."

I sure hate having had to let him go. I can hear the thoughts of people telling me to get over it. Why should I be so sad? I just laughed as I wrote that. Look how long I got to have him in my life. What a great privilege. So, he didn't get to see me have kids. That doesn't mean I won't or that he won't be an influence on them. Also, if what I believe really is true, how much better for him to be, at the proper time, with God? I believe Fr. Francis Hoffman, the Relevant Radio priest, was quoting St. José Maria Escriva when he said that, at the time of death, God does not come as a stalking hunter but as a cultivating gardener, plucking us at just the right time. Isn't that amazing? God is outside of time; He created it. When you're conceived, you enter in time; when you die, you are out of time. You enter into forever now, eternity. The gardener has come. It's about time.

I took that rosary with me to San Francisco. Because it touched the first-class relic of Blessed Solanus Casey, it is a third-class relic. Brother Pascal said to let them know if anything miraculous happened from touching Dad with it. You already know nothing did. Although I did witness a miracle the day before at Mass in the Cathedral of the Assumption of Mary, when the priest said the prayer and bread and wine became the body, blood, soul, and divinity of Jesus Christ. I did touch Dad with that rosary on the chest and forehead and hugged him and cried with Mom as I led her in the rosary, the Litany of the Blessed Virgin Mary, and the Solanus Casey canonization prayer, followed by the Divine Mercy Chaplet. When we started the Chaplet is when we allowed them to turn off the life support. His body hadn't been responding any more. He lasted around seventeen minutes, I believe. It's really sad, but it's still fortunate, a great father who was a devoted husband, who protected and served Mom for fifty-one years, seven months and seven days. A priceless gift from God. For the previous twenty-one years, he sang in the church choir, and he told me this was his way of being close to his own mother—a choir singer and professional cantor—after she died.

I start every day praying that rosary. I kiss each bead and the crucifix and the etchings of Jesus and Mary as I go through it. As I kneel in my kitchen for the prayer, I face a crucifix on the cabinet to my left and a picture of me and Dad outside the Cathedral of Saint Paul, wearing our Ancient Order of Hibernian sashes after St. Patrick's Day Mass, on the refrigerator to my right. The last thing with which I ever touched Dad. That's my way of being with him. That's how I start every day. No, touching him with that rosary before our prayers didn't get him out of bed, and doing a dance, it just sent him on his way, with love, to God, the perfect Gardener, who plucks us back to him at just the right time.

We flew back home on Friday, October 4. The visitation was Monday, October 14, the funeral, burial, and wake on Tuesday, October 15. Dad got the Rifle Squad Gun Salute, and Mom was presented the American flag and the empty shell casings. Later, Representative Betty McCollum sent another flag, one that had been flown in his honor outside the Capitol building in Washington, D.C., along with a letter to Mom honoring him for his advocacy for U.S. military veterans. The Friday before he died, while watching him on life support, Mom actually answered a call to Dad's mobile phone from McCollum's aide, asking if he would be making his appointment at one o'clock that day to discuss veterans' issues with her. That's how he lived, always on to the next thing, giving of himself, doing the best he could and making the most out of every day. As David said, Dad died at seventy-four and one-half years, but he packed about one hundred and fifty years into them.

I was slowly getting back into the swing of things, picking up personal training business at the gym, which had finally completely moved to the larger space at the other end of the building. There were two rings, and I was walking the apron on the north side of the smaller one, which was wood-framed and homemade, standing about a foot and a half up from the floor, watching the twenty-one-year-old son of a high school classmate of mine shadowbox under my direction. He was throwing good combinations, and I was encouraging him as I got a few feet away from the opposite corner, when my right foot, coming down on a spot where the edge of the padding beneath the canvas was uneven, slipped off, and the outer edge of my shoe hit the concrete floor with all my weight behind it, turning the bottom of my foot inward and perfectly parallel to my right leg, the rest of my body crashing down. I thought my ankle was broken as I loudly moaned in pain, slowly picking myself up and realizing I could not walk. I had lightly torn a couple of ligaments, which would take months of rest, followed by physical therapy. So, the end of 2019 and the beginning of 2020 was a time of recovery. I had just started running again when the shutdown happened. I was feeling better but nowhere near to being back in shape when the riots started.

The first night of guarding buildings after the riots broke out, at one point, my former Aín Dah Yung colleague, David Goodman, had me drive him and two other guys to the AIM barricade on Cedar Avenue and East 24th Street, between Little Earth housing project on the southeast corner at Cedar Avenue and Holy Rosary on the southwest corner of 18th Avenue South, a mini-block west. David verified the spot was secure and got radio communication to head up to Division of Indian Works on East Lake Street and 10th Avenue. The parking lot entrance on the west end of that property is directly across the street from the U.S. Bank building burnt up the night before. AIM had prevented DIW from also being lit on fire that night, and they intended to protect it again. Police had diverted a demonstration eastward from Chicago Avenue a couple of blocks up, and they needed more protectors in front of the DIW building. Everything was fine. We stood staring down some young tough guys walking by, making eye contact, then after a nod, they walked on. These three happened to be black guys, young and big and strong. I wasn't brandishing a gun, nor was David or the other guys with us, so they didn't know if we were armed or not, although my hand was in my pocket gripping a pistol, my body language suggesting the probability. I got this powerful feeling, like some probable arsonists were frightened away by me, then I realized about five guys, who were all twice my size, were right behind me with rifles and a baseball bat. Also, who knows what the three men were up to? You have a right to demonstrate, and really, that's all they were doing. For all I knew, in a different context, we'd be hanging out together.

Holy Rosary was protected during the riots because it's across the street from Little Earth, and AIM Patrol wasn't letting anything happen in their neighborhood. That's the Phillips neighborhood, where the diverse group of residents coordinated over the summer their own patrols of specific blocks to stop crime that picked up immediately after the riots, because the police were barely responding if they were even able to do so. Saint Albert the Great Catholic Church, also in South Minneapolis, was protected by AIM Patrol. Their former Catholic grade school is now an American Indian charter school, and so they cooperated with each other as one community. The last three nights of patrolling, I spent the critical overnight hours on the roof of the All Nations Indian Church, a United Church of Christ building on East 23rd Street and Bloomington Avenue. I remembered good friends while alone on that building, listening to the traditional drumming and singing going on four blocks east at Little Earth as I looked at the night sky. I wondered how Dad would feel about me doing this, knowing he'd approve, knowing he'd trust that

I would be responsible and cautious with the carrying of any weapon and level-headed about any confrontation, keeping in mind that I was protecting my own home while a guest and a servant to a community welcoming me as a relative. I thought of how I'd been called to service by Darwin Strong, a security guard at Little Earth in his younger years, who had been a Marine, too young for the Vietnam War, serving in the late '70s, early '80s. I thought of how our faiths were different, but we'd been in the center of each other's religious observance over the years, Darwin having attended—and much of the time suffered through—St. Joseph's Boarding School in South Dakota and Gabby, being on her Dad's side Italian from Queens, New York. I thought of that first Sundance with them in Kyle, when Gabby had me accompany her daughter, Gianna, three or four years old, up to the circle where she and Darwin carried her to the Cottonwood tree. Darwin later told me how she had started to cry and how he told her, "It's okay, sweetheart; this is how we pray. Remember? This is how we pray," and she was calm, and they prayed. Not too different from when Dad calmed me at Mass, and I listened to the priest tell us how God is always calling us to Him and how we are always longing for Him.

I thought of that those nights. These are my friends. Dad had died. After that, everything went crazy. No, the third-class Solanus Casey relic rosary did not save Dad's earthly life in a miracle, but that doesn't mean God wouldn't have done it if it were in His plan. Just like how Steve DuBray, when closing the 2003 Sundance after everyone else was gone and we in the Helper's Camp prayed with him while he smoked his Peace Pipe with us, explained that the relative we'd been praying for that Sundance had died. Sometimes, God will save the life of someone we're praying for, but sometimes, it's just His will for that person to come home to Him, and we have to accept it, just like Fr. Rocky explained, when the perfect Gardener is ready to pick you from His garden.

I've had so many dreams and ambitions, mostly connected to boxing and writing, most of which are still inside of me, never fully articulated or lived out in the world. For decades, I've thought my wheels have only been spinning, but little by little, I've been interacting with people, with my fellow Americans, in a land I hope we can keep sovereign and sane and prevent from falling into the dictatorship of relativism. Yes, Holy Rosary and St. Albert the Great were protected, but someone did try to burn down the Basilica of St. Mary in downtown Minneapolis. In California, New York, Denver, and all across the country, Catholic churches and statues have been vandalized, and in Florida, one man even tried to burn down a church with people in it. This has happened in France and in Central and South America, too. Just before the Rwanda genocide, such vandalism of Catholic churches was also happening. AIM Patrol has the right idea: protect your people in an uncompromising and respectful way.

Today I finish this book. It is Monday, March 29, 2021, the Monday of Holy Week. Next week, after the Easter Triduum, we will celebrate the fifty days of Easter, and time will keep moving right along, whether you do or not. Dad was right years ago when he asked me why I hadn't completed at least five books by then. I'd been thinking it myself, although as a son, I didn't want to hear it from him. Or actually, I did want to hear it and needed to hear it because that was the responsible way to love me, but I was too prideful to discuss it. As I said earlier, he was always right. I confessed the argument to the priest, who'd been my high school religion teacher senior year, although he never knew, because it was behind the screen in the confessional. He gave me three prayers to pray for Dad that I still pray every day. That got me praying for other fathers, like my brother and my cousins, like all my friends with kids, like my far away friend, Bob Dildine, like the priests and the Pope, like my friends Darwin and Art and Ray, and yes, friends like David Goodman and others who, like me, at least to this point, don't have kids but are working with kids all the time. Yeah, all the time until I'm out of time.

Speaking of being out of time, which I know is closer for me every day, I'm writing now when I have the time because right now is the only time. I've finished this book. After Dad died, I cried and cried and cried. I lamented him not being alive to see me married, to see me have kids, and to see me publish my first book. He did see me get published with many articles and two poems, *My Now Departed Brother* and *Upon the Finishing of My House Fried Rice*. I believe there are about twenty poems in this short book. Just as Dad had suggested, it's time to get over myself and get my book completed and move on to the next one. I know you, the reader of this book, are one in a million, at least, but that doesn't guarantee a million are going to buy the book. Preferably, more will! No matter, if I fall flat on my face as I suggested I could in the beginning, I'll just do better next time. I have that stolen novel to revise and that play to revise and turn into a novella and more stories to write and a trilogy I'm foreseeing, but you'll never get to read them if I don't end this book and spend time on the next one. So that's what I intend to do, right now. It's about time.

About the Author

Mark Connor is a Literary Pugilist from Saint Paul, Minnesota. A lifelong boxer and Boxing Trainer, he runs a service called, Fighting Chance/Boxing For Life. His writing about Boxing, as well as his training services, can be found at https://BoxersAndWritersMagazine.com. He writes fiction, poetry, and journalism. He is the 2022 Boxing inductee to the Mancini's St. Paul Sports Hall of Fame. He attended the University of St. Thomas in Saint Paul, Regis University in Denver, Colorado, and graduated with a BA in English from the University of Minnesota. He has written and published many articles about Boxing, Irish culture, and people and events related to Irish freedom. He has also published local news and features on business, politics, and current affairs in Minnesota and the U.S. His Substack newsletter, *Irish, Catholic, Punchdrunk in Saint Paul*, can be found at https://markconnoricpunchdrunk.substack.com.

www.ingramcontent.com/pod-product-compliance
Lightning Source LLC
Chambersburg PA
CBHW071202090426
42736CB00012B/2419